NEEDED TRUTH 2012 (VOLUME 119)

Published by:

HAYES PRESS Publisher, Resources & Media,

The Barn, Flaxlands

Royal Wootton Bassett

Swindon, SN4 8DY

United Kingdom

www.hayespress.org

JESUS CHRIST: (1) THE RADIANCE OF GOD'S GLORY (DAVID WOODS)

On a recent holiday, I enjoyed the pleasure of an early morning jog. As the country roads turned towards the east, the low position of the sun in the winter sky made it difficult to see anything else in front of me. The brightness of the sun on that clear morning was blinding, and care was needed to ensure I didn't run into oncoming traffic or some obstacles that could trip me up. It was glorious, yet, at the same time, a little uncomfortable!

On a Galilee mountain the disciples Peter, James and John had an experience that was even more glorious. Shortly before they climbed that mountain to pray with Jesus, Peter had declared that he and the other disciples were convinced that Jesus was the Christ, the promised Messiah and the Son of the Living God.[1] There, on that mountaintop, it was as if God wanted to confirm that fact unmistakably, and Jesus' face and form was changed in a unique way. Matthew tells us, *he was transfigured before them, and his face shone like the sun, and his clothes became white as light.*[1] Jesus Christ shone brighter than the sun! Something of His heavenly glory, that was His from all eternity,[3] burst through and astounded those men. In Heb.1:3 we're told that *He is the radiance of the glory of God.* Forever, God's Son has been radiating and shining forth as the glory of God.

David could write in Ps.19:1, *The heavens declare the glory of God.* He was awestruck as he viewed, without the aid of modern telescopes, the grandeur of God's creation and the stars that filled the night sky. For him they declared the glory of God. And the vast universe that we can peer into today still does the same! But the heavens are not the glory of

Table of Contents

God; they are only a declaration of God's glory, which is far and above anything that He has created. God's glory is His alone!

It's useful to try to define 'glory'. A suggested definition is: 'God's glory is the beauty of His manifold perfections. It can refer to the bright and awesome radiance that sometimes breaks forth in visible manifestations. Or it can refer to the infinite moral excellence of His character. In either case it signifies a reality of infinite greatness and worth.' [4] In Heb.1:3 the Greek word *(doxa)* that's translated 'glory' has the sense of 'something, or someone that owns a high estimation or opinion, and therefore has honour that results from that good opinion.'[5] Realising that the glory of God we are considering in this scripture is the 'infinite excellence of His character', we come to appreciate that God the Son is the radiance of the unparalleled and unmatched being, person and character of God.

This brings us, for a moment, into the mind-bending truth of the Godhead: God who is one, yet three distinct persons - God the Father, God the Son and God the Holy Spirit - who are entirely and completely God in themselves! Jesus said that, *"God is spirit..."* [6] and John declared that *no one has ever seen God; the only God, who is at the Father's side, he has made him known.*[7] So, we're right to think that it's God the Father being referred to, *whom no one has ever seen or can see.* [8] Yet, by the grace of God, we're able to see and know God, and His glory, through the person of God the Son, and the working of God the Holy Spirit, who indwells all believers.[9] We are helped by God Himself to understand something of the true magnitude of what we're considering here: that being fully God, God the Son radiates everything that God is in His infinite being and person.

Radiance means a 'shining forth', or the 'light that shines from a luminous body'.[10] Just like the bright sun radiates a blinding light by virtue of what it is, so God the Son radiates the awesome glory of God by virtue of who He is. And He has done so for all eternity, and will continue to do so for all eternity! Isaiah and Ezekiel had awesome visions of heaven, and they both saw one like a man on the throne in heaven. It was a glorious sight that was almost beyond description,[11]but they were looking at Him who is the radiance of God's glory, the eternal Son of God. And this was prior to His *being born in the likeness of men ... being found in human form.*[12] Now we stand in awe of the grand plans of God, that He would reveal Himself and His glory to us, through God the eternal Son, by His taking on human flesh.

God had declared something of His glory in the creation of the universe. He had declared something of His glory through the giving of the Law and the Word of God that today comprises our Old Testaments. But that wasn't enough. God the Son, the one who is the radiance of the glory of God, walked on this earth with us. *And the Word became flesh and dwelt among us, and we have seen his glory, glory as of the only Son from the Father, full of grace and truth.*[13] This was the full expression of God's glory to us.

In everything He was excellent. He was infinitely better than any who had lived before, and any of His contemporaries. He is superior in all ways to any who have lived since. He was sinless perfection,[14] and He exuded the character of God in all that He did, while subjecting and humbling Himself to the limitations of human experience. Peter, recounting his experience on that mountaintop, wrote that *he received honour and glory from God the Father, and the voice was borne to him by the Majestic Glory, "This is my beloved Son, with whom I am well pleased," we ourselves heard this very voice borne from heaven, for we were with him on the holy mountain.*[15] God declared from heaven on three occasions His delight in God the Son, the one who became the Son of

Man, who was the radiance of the glory of God in every aspect of His life.

John wrote that the Lord's first miracle, changing water into wine at the wedding parts in Cana. *manifested his glory,*[16] Through the wonder of His countless miracles, the glory of God was also seen. He is the radiance of the glory of God. There is none that compares to Him, and to what He has done. But there was more that the Lord Jesus wanted His disciples to know about the eternal glory of God. He prayed the night before Calvary, *"Father, I desire **that they** also, whom you have given me, may be with me where I am, to see my glory [doxa] that you have given me because you loved me before the foundation of the world."*[17] For all eternity, those who are His will delight in Him who will forever be the radiance of the glory of God. It's through the person of our Lord Jesus Christ that we will be eternally introduced to the beauty of God's manifold perfections.

It required the eternal Son to humble Himself *by becoming obedient to the point of death, even death on a cross,*[18] so that we sinners, who had fallen so far short of recognising and acknowledging God's glory,[19] might be brought into the *light of the knowledge of the glory of God in the face of Jesus Christ.*[20] Later in Hebrews we're encouraged to run, *looking to Jesus, the founder and perfecter of our faith, who for the joy that was set before him endured the cross, despising the shame, and is seated at the right hand of the throne of God.*[21] Running and looking to Him who is the radiance of the glory of God, should be a glorious experience. Dark shadows are cast on us when something comes between the Son and us. What things are casting shadows in our lives and block our view of the glory of God as we see it in the face of Jesus? Remove them!

In the clear, unobstructed light of His infinite perfections and eternal excellence, things that are of fleeting and fading value must be put in their proper place. There is nothing and no one to compare to our God, and the one who is the radiance of His glory. Enjoy Him now, and for ever.

References: (1) Matt.16:16 (2) Matt.17:2 (3) Jn 17:5 (4) J. Piper, Desiring God: Meditations of a Christian Hedonist, 2004 (5) W.E. Vine, Vine's Expository Dictionary of Old & New Testament Words: Glory, Glorious (6) Jn 4:24 (7) Jn 1:18 (8) 1 Tim.6:16 (9) Rom.8:9,11 (10) W.E. Vine, Vine's Expository Dictionary of Old & New Testament Words: Bright, Brightness (11) see Isa.6 and Ezek.1 (12) Phil.2:7-8 (13) Jn 1:14 (14) 1 Jn 3:5 (15) 2 Pet.1:17-18 (16) Jn 2:11 (17) Jn 17:24 (18) Phil.2:8 (19) Rom.3:23 (20) 2 Cor.4:6 (21) Heb.12:2

Bible quotations from ESV

JESUS CHRIST: (2) THE EXACT IMPRINT OF GOD'S NATURE (KARL SMITH)

Last time we looked at the description of the Lord Jesus in Heb.1:3 as *the radiance of the glory of God,* This phrase focuses on how the Lord Jesus shines out one particular aspect of God: His 'glory'. Now we move on to how the Lord Jesus expresses all of God's innermost being: His 'nature'. *He is ... the exact imprint of his <u>nature</u>,* the writer to the Hebrews continues in the English Standard Version. The Revised version chooses the word 'substance' instead of 'nature'. The Greek word both are trying to translate is *hypostasis.* This was a word that had been used four hundred years or so beforehand by Plato and other Greek philosophers to mean the real nature of something, underlying its appearance.

Readers familiar with C.S. Lewis's Narnia series will remember the description of heaven that appears at the end of the final book in the series, *The Last Battle.* In his fictitious universe, Lewis imagines heaven to be a larger and perfected version of the places they have loved throughout their lives. Perhaps fancifully, the book explains that the England the characters had lived in before their death and the Narnia known by those who had lived there were merely shadow lands, which give physical expression to the real England and the real Narnia that exist as part of the real world above. 'The reason why we loved the old Narnia is that it sometimes looks a little like this', a unicorn rapturously explains to the children. Their friend the Professor replies, "It's all in Plato, all in Plato: bless me, what *do* they teach them at these schools!"

Plato, in his *Republic,* compared the world to a cave whose inhabitants see only distorted shadows, thrown on the roof by a crackling fire, of what is really there in the larger world outside. The external material things we can see are bound to be illusionary in some way in Plato's thought, just like the shadows in the cave. Underlying each one, however, is an inner nature, its substance, its reality. One of the words Plato uses for this is its *hypostasis,* the same word translated 'nature' or 'substance' in Heb.1:3.

The nature or substance of something, then, is no woolly theory about it, but something solid you could rely on if only you could grasp it. The word literally means 'underneath standing' and this signals how foundational it is. In fact, by the time of the New Testament, the Greek word had come to mean an absolute confidence in the thing under discussion and it is used in this way later on in Hebrews e.g. *Now faith is the assurance* [this time the Authorised Version *does* translate this word as 'substance'] *of things hoped for.*[1] But how can we with our tiny finite minds ever hope to grasp the nature of God firmly enough to have this kind of confidence in Him?

He wanted to make His invisible nature visible to us. He sent us more than a flickering shadow. In fact, He sent His Son who is *the exact imprint* of *his nature.* The New International Version (NIV) translates this word as *the exact representation of His being.* Other scriptures such as 2 Cor.4:4 and Col.1:15 talk about the Lord Jesus as *the image of God* and *the image of the invisible God.* In these verses the Holy Spirit chooses the word *eikon,* which we still use in English as 'icon'. This emphasises the visual element of what is seen, something you can look at. Heb.1:3 uses a deeper word, which is found only once in our Bibles, *charakter.* This word, by contrast, emphasises the process by which the image is made. It was a symbol created by an engraving tool on something like a coin. Or perhaps a seal on a ring was pressed in hot wax. When it cooled down, the image left in it would show exactly what was on the seal. We still use this word in a similar way. In printing, a character such as a letter or number on the page reflects exactly what is on the head of the typewriter or on the printing press. To take yet another example, by looking at the imprint in the snow, you can see exactly the pattern of the boot that has walked in it.

The Lord Jesus is not a rough approximation, a vague idea of what God is like. He is not a shadow of God's nature, as in Plato's cave. Shadows lengthen out at twilight and shrink in towards mid-day. They dance and move in bizarre ways as the fire crackles. He is not someone from whom we can piece together a good guess as to God's nature. The unfathomable nature of God is represented **exactly** in His Son, *the exact imprint of his nature.* This happens to an extent in human families. We carry genetic information in our DNA that often causes us to resemble our parents, whether in looks or character. How often have you heard someone say, "So and so is the image of his father"? No-one looks precisely identical to his father, however. We all have features of our own to add to the mix.

The Lord Jesus is the express image of His Father's substance with nothing added into the mix from elsewhere. Of all the 'many ways' God had spoken through the prophets mentioned in Heb.1, none had been so precise an expression of His being as this expression *in these last days* when *he has spoken to us by his Son.*[2] This, however, is not to downplay the Old Testament Scriptures. They form part of the divine Word of God as the main means by which we learn about who God is today. As our inner thoughts need words to communicate them to others, so the Bible communicates the truth of God to us perfectly and directly. Because of the limitations of our human languages and our finite minds, however, God sent His Son to communicate, not only His truth, but His whole nature. Many of those who saw Him would not be able to read the Scriptures, although they could hear them read aloud. Nevertheless, the Lord Jesus was a walking, talking Bible to them in His actions and personality as much as in His teaching. It is no accident that the Lord Jesus is also called 'The Word'.[3]

Looking at the Lord Jesus is precisely equivalent to looking at God. That's why He could tell Philip, *"Whoever has seen me has seen the Father".*[4] I suspect that the angels in heaven cannot directly see or even understand the nature of God, but perhaps even there He delights in revealing it through His Son. Certainly, however, God was seen through His Son on earth. Those who saw Him act saw the way God acts: *"the Son can do nothing of his own accord, but only what he sees the Father doing. For whatever the Father does, that the Son does likewise."*[5] He gave the example of raising the dead, something only God could do.[6] Soon Jairus's daughter and Lazarus would be able to testify that the Son was the image of the Father in this respect, making God's power to raise the dead spectacularly visible. We look forward to the day when He will raise our loved ones who have died in Christ - and then ourselves - to enjoy eternal life in new bodies. Equally they could be confident that the teaching they heard from Him was not different by a single syllable from what God Himself wanted to teach them: *"I do nothing on my own authority, but speak just as the Father taught me."*[7]

Some aspects of God's nature as expressed in Christ shocked enemy and disciple alike, such as the profound holiness that extended beyond external things into the hidden motives - and also the consuming desire to extend forgiveness to even the most unpalatable of people. *"Who can forgive sins but God alone?"* asked the scribes, not realising that God's exact imprint was among them.[8] Their concept of God's nature was too small. Human philosophy cannot comprehend its fullness in words and concepts, so God sent His Son for us to see it expressed in a person, *For in him the whole fullness of deity dwells bodily.*[9]

References: (1) Heb.11:1 (2) Heb.1:1-2 (3) Jn 1:1-14 (4) Jn 14:9 (5) Jn 5:19 (6) Jn 5:21 (7) Jn 8:28 (8) Mk.2:7 (9) Col.2:9

Bible quotations from ESV

JESUS CHRIST: (3) THE UPHOLDER OF ALL THINGS (STEPHEN HICKLING)

By faith we understand that the worlds were prepared by the word of God...[1]

This takes us right back to the beginning, to Gen.1. It was by the mouth of God that the universe was created and we know that the creation was effected through the Son. Whilst Heb.11:3 has the command of God in **creative** power in view, however, Heb.1:3 focuses on the Son's word of **sustaining** power: *The Son ... sustaining all things by his powerful word.*[2]

'Sustaining' conveys the dual thought of support and movement. By His every word, God the Son not only upholds the universe, but regulates it and carries it forward. His powerful imperative is the reason the universe both exists as it does and continues to exist.

For by [or in] Him all things were created, both in the heavens and on earth, visible and invisible, whether thrones or dominions or rulers or authorities — all things have been created through Him and for Him. He is before all things, and in Him all things hold together.[3]

In Col.1, the Lord's priority and authority, vis-a-vis His creation, are clear: all things were created by Him and for Him. More than that, though, all things were created **in** Him. That seems to express something of the dependence which the creation has on the Lord. It is solely on account of all things being the result of His creative design, will and continued supply of energy that our universe hangs together as it does. Don't the laws of nature bear out so clearly the harmony and solidarity of the Godhead and testify also to the Son's tireless work of upholding? And yet, what a marked contrast we see in the 'upholder of all things', as He was led away to be crucified. We read of Him: *Then they brought Him to the place Golgotha, which is translated, Place of a Skull.* [4]

The same word, which is used of His upholding power in Heb.1:3, is here used of the men who 'brought' Him to Golgotha. Of course, they had no knowledge of the sustaining power of the One they bore. They saw a man exhausted from trial and false testimony, battered by the scourging of Roman soldiers, and agonising at what He alone knew lay before Him; and so they carried Him to the Place of the Skull. We rejoice at the grace of God in allowing the 'upholder of all things' to be brought by sinful men to Calvary! Yet, physically weakened though the Saviour was (struggling even to 'uphold' His own cross - see Lk.23:26), how thankful we are that *He himself bore our sins in his body on the tree, so that we might die to sins and live for righteousness.* [5] He carried a weight far greater at Calvary than the cross of wood he carried to Calvary. In God's mercy, we will never know how heavy that cup of God's wrath against sin was; He bore it on the cross, where He drained it completely, even to the very dregs.

By His powerful word

The Lord Jesus is the Word (Gk. *'logos'*) that was with God, that was God and that became flesh.[6] *'Logos'* means the expression of thought and, as the Word, Christ is the full expression of the heart and mind of God. In His person, character and actions, He fully communicates to us all that we are able to comprehend about God. In Heb.1:3, though, the focus is on the detail of His every utterance (Gk. *'Rhema'*). The words He speaks are full of power to sustain; they uphold the universe!

The power of divine utterance was evident in creation. God spoke and it was so and He saw that it was good. Just so, the words of the Lord

Jesus carry dynamic force. After all, He told His disciples that He did not speak on His own, but spoke only what He was commanded to speak by His Father. Even the words He used were the ones His Father gave Him to speak and time after time in the gospel narratives we see their wonderful power. The Jews often expressed the power of God in their writings by phrases such as 'He carries all His creatures' or 'He bears His world'. The writer to the Hebrews was giving clear testimony to the deity of the Lord Jesus, then, in stating that by His powerful words, the Lord sustains all things. What a striking contrast there is between the power of man and the power of God: man demonstrates his power by acts of great exertion, by force and by violence; yet it is characteristic of God alone that He need only speak to work wonders.

For nothing will be impossible with God.[7]

Literally, this verse tells us that no word (Gk. *rhema)* of God shall be without power. The Lord never wastes a word. Everything He says is vitally important and never fails to accomplish the purposes for which it is spoken. As disciples of the Lord Jesus, we would do well to hang on His every word, for not one of them will return to Him void. Of course, the whole Bible is the inspired Word of God, but many of us will have Bibles which emphasise the spoken words of the Lord Jesus in some way (perhaps highlighting them with the use of red text). Time spent in the gospels, studying the records of the Lord Jesus' sayings will be time well-spent.

Eph.6 contains the passage of Scripture which talks about the Christian's armour: those things with which we should clothe ourselves daily if we are to withstand the attacks of the evil one. *And take the helmet of salvation, and the sword of the Spirit, which is the word of God.*[8] 'Word' here is *'rhema'* - we need a firm grip on the individual words or sayings of God if we're to succeed in our spiritual warfare. For those of us in the west, the Word of God is freely available. Many of us will carry the whole Bible in our pockets on our PDAs and smartphones; the words of the Lord are at our fingertips. There is, however, still great benefit to be had in memorising these words. How much better-equipped for battle will we be with small phrases and verses committed to memory! We need only recall the Lord's temptation in the wilderness to answer that question. God desires that we learn His words and He will enable us, by His Spirit, to do so if we patiently dedicate time to this exercise.

Our Lord Jesus Christ is the sustainer of all things: all things live, breathe and have their being in Him. How much more inclined is He to bear up those He calls His own! Shouldn't the security of the everlasting arms evoke a desire in us to pay close attention to His words? His are the words of abundant life; if they abide in us, those words will empower us to live in the freedom for which we were saved, rather than as slaves again to things from which He died to set us free.

References: (1) Heb.11:3 (2) Heb.1:3 NIV (3) Col.1:16-17 (4) Mk.15:22 (5) 1 Pet.2:24 NIV (6) Jn 1:1,14 (7) Lk.1:37 (8) Eph.6:17

Bible quotations from NASB unless otherwise stated

JESUS CHRIST: (4) THE PURIFIER OF SINS WHO HAS SAT DOWN ON HIGH (DON WILLIAMSON)

The writers of this series have been presenting the wonders of our exalted Christ. He is the eternal Son of God, the one appointed heir of all things, the one through whom the worlds are made! The verse we have been looking at in Heb.1:3 reveals: *He is the radiance of God's glory, and the exact representation of God's nature.* Can we ever understand or truly appreciate the scriptural statement that says, *He upholds all things by the word of His power?* Our Saviour is the exalted one; none can compare with Him, and it is in this context that we are to consider the fact that He is the purifier of sins.

Purification of the flesh

In order to appreciate what our Lord Jesus has done for us it might be good to see what was required by God in Old Testament times for dealing with this issue of sin. We actually find one of the best explanations in the New Testament, in the book of Hebrews: *For if the blood of goats and bulls, and the sprinkling of defiled persons with the ashes of a heifer, sanctify for the purification of the flesh, how much more will the blood of Christ, who through the eternal Spirit offered himself without blemish to God, purify our conscience from dead works to serve the living God.* [1] Sin has been the separator from the beginning of time. God's provision for dealing with it in order for man to continue to have a relationship with Him was the offering of sacrifices (from a pure heart), resulting in *the purification of the flesh.*

This was to be at a cost to the one who had sinned and of course, it was the ultimate cost to the sacrifice that was offered in place of the sinner. The power in the verse of Hebrews that we read is seen in the contrast of the sacrifices of the past to the one who is our once-for-all sacrifice. We get to consider the words, 'how much more'. There is no comparison between the one who is the purifier of sins and the possibly millions of animal sacrifices offered in the past. As I have already stated, there is none to compare with Him! This is what brings us to the point of wonder, that one of such exalted place should lower Himself to face the judgment and punishment due to us, so that we can serve God as those who have been cleansed.

Refined by fire

I'm sure we can all understand the fact that some things are refined or purified by fire. While water is the usual symbol of cleansing, fire can be too; John's comments about the Lord baptizing in fire may illustrate this;[2] and there is also the passage that commanded the Israelites to: *purify yourselves and your captives ... and all articles ... everything that can stand the fire, you shall pass through the fire ... And whatever cannot stand the fire, you shall pass through the water.* [3] Although there are many metals that go through this process to reach their highest quality of purification, the best example might be gold. In order to secure the quality and high price of gold all foreign particles must be removed, and it is the application of fire that separates the pure gold from all the rest. Perhaps Peter had this cleansing in mind, when commenting on the practical outworking of the purification the Lord accomplishes.[4]

The Lord acknowledges this process in an illustrative point to the Church in Laodicea. *You say, I am rich, I have prospered, and I need nothing, not realizing that you are wretched, pitiable, poor, blind, and naked. I counsel you to buy from me gold refined by fire, so that you may be rich, and white garments so that you may clothe yourself ...* [5] The saints in Laodicea had missed the mark, as they were neither hot nor cold toward God, but rather they were lukewarm. In fact, they were content to say that they were rich in this world's goods and therefore needed nothing. Yet the reality was they were spiritually poor and if they were to become truly rich they were to buy from Him spiritual riches refined by fire and white righteous garments of spiritual living. The riches of a man are what he is and does rather than what he has. The Lord knew all about the cost of the refining process and still He was willing to go through the pain and suffering of Calvary knowing that He would face the fierce judgment from a holy God and shed His blood so that you and I might have the purification of our sins.

Some of you may have heard of the forest fires in Colorado during this summer. We have had fires every year so in some ways it was not new, but this time the winds pushed the fire into a large city and the result was 365 homes being burnt to the ground. As I drove past the city that night on my way back to Littleton from Trinidad, I was awestruck with the sight of the fires on the side of the hills and on the edge of the city as house after house exploded in flame. A few days later, with the fires out, photos showed the total devastation and destruction that was left behind. Empty driveways and concrete foundations were all that were remaining in an entire neighbourhood. It is a reminder of the purging power of fire. Our series aims to bring into our consciousness a fresh appreciation of Christ as the preeminent one without peer [6] and, at the same time, rejoicing that we have a relationship with Him by grace.

Who has sat down on high

The statement in Hebrews takes us from Christ being the purifier of sins to being the one who has *sat down ...on high*. When we are contemplating the person and work of the Lord Jesus, we should always remember that our Saviour is the ultimate victor! Think for a moment about the other religions of this world. Mohammad was a prophet, but he is dead and buried; Buddhism encompasses a variety of traditions, beliefs and practices largely based on teachings attributed to

Siddhartha Gautama, who is commonly known as the Buddha, a man who has also died. And many of the cults like Mormonism and Jehovah's Witnesses all follow men who have died.

You and I serve a living Saviour, one who has conquered sin, death and Satan's power and is now at the right hand of the throne of the Majesty in heaven![7] The description we are considering is one of position and authority, and from the view of a completed work. This should thrill our hearts as we realise the place the Lord occupies in the heavens for us, knowing that He is there as our High Priest, a minister in the holy places on our behalf. What a transformational change from sacrifice to High Priest!

As we think in awe of our Lord and Saviour, it would be good to go back and focus for a moment on the saints in Laodicea. The Lord said He would 'spit them out of His mouth' for being lukewarm.[8] It must have grieved the Lord's heart, knowing the place He had left to come for men, the place He took on our behalf and the place of His ascended power. But He says to them, *"Those whom I love, I reprove and discipline, so be zealous and repent... The one who conquers, I will grant him to sit with Me on My throne, as I also conquered and sat down with My Father on His throne."* [9] Wow! What a Saviour we have, one who by His grace has saved us from the eternal fire of judgement, purifies us for service before God, and seeks to share with us His glorious throne! Can we compare the riches of this world with Him? May we all seek to buy (for it will cost us time and convenience) of His gold, and to put on the garments of His holiness, for we are to be holy as He is holy.[10]

"He who has an ear, let him hear what the Spirit says to the churches." [11]

Bible quotations from ESV

References: (1) Heb.9:13-14 (2) Lk.3:16; cf. Mk.10:38-39 (3) Num.31:19-23 (4) 1 Pet.1:3-9 (5) Rev.3:17-18 (6) Col.3:15-20 (7) Heb.8:1 (8) Rev.3:16 (9) Rev.3:19-21 (10) 1 Pet.1:16 (11) Rev.3:22

JESUS CHRIST: (5) THE MESSIAH – THE SUPREMACY OF THE SON (KEITH DORRICOTT)

For most of this world's history, Christ the Son of God has been invisible to mankind. Even when, almost two thousand years ago, He came into this world as 'Jesus' for a short while, He was in effect in disguise; His supreme visible glory was hidden.[1] Most people developed wrong notions about who He was, despite the unique evidence of what He did, as Isaiah the prophet had written about long before.[2] This evidence was confirmed to John the Baptist, who was looking for Him at the time.[3] And so there were relatively few who were able to see Him then as the one who was clearly superior to all others.

But one day in the future He will come back here in His visible majestic glory - which He now possesses as a glorified man in heaven. Every eye will see Him at that time[4] and know exactly who He is. Every knee will bow down and honour Him for who He is.[5] And everyone's tongue will confess the fact that He is indeed Lord of all.[6] There will be no exceptions. For He is the one and only Messiah (the 'Christ') promised by God from long ago[7] - the one uniquely chosen and anointed by God and consecrated by Him to be king and priest. Although He has already been given all authority in heaven and on earth,[8] He does not yet exercise it over those people who are not willingly subject to Him; instead, He holds it back - but only for a time. All who are opposed to Him will most certainly be put under His complete rule by His Father;[9] after He will yet come to earth in full glory. Of this there is no doubt.

His qualification

Why Christ? Why does He get this supreme honour? The reason is that He has clearly demonstrated that He is, by far, the most qualified for it - in fact the only one. The epistle to the Hebrews makes His qualification very clear, and describes Him categorically as being superior to all others. It shows, for example, that He is greater than Moses, who was exemplary as a faithful servant in the house of God on earth, the tabernacle constructed in the wilderness; however, it was only temporary, and just a reflection of the true one.[10] Christ is forever Son over God's true house.

It shows how He is superior to Joshua as a leader, who took the people of Israel into their Promised Land after Moses, but was not able to bring them all the way to Mount Zion, God's chosen place for His people to worship Him then.[11] Christ has brought us into God with no barrier or distance left.[12] And it shows that He is superior to Aaron, Israel's first high priest[13] who established the priestly order of Aaron for others to follow under the old covenant. However, the law of that covenant could never bring people all the way to God; there was always a barrier because of sin - which Christ removed by the sacrifice of Himself.[14] And, more than that, the Hebrews' epistle begins by showing how He is also vastly superior to the highest rank and capability of created beings: angels.

There are immense multitudes of angelic beings,[15] they have great power which they use in God's service, and some of them serve in the very presence of God.[16] They are His messengers and agents, but they are limited in how they can carry this out. But the Son has no such limitations. As Jesus Himself said: "... *no one knows the Son except the*

Father, and no one knows the Father except the Son and anyone to whom the Son chooses to reveal him." [17]

When He came initially in the flesh, He was willingly subjected for a while to a lower place than angels occupy, [18] to become a man in order to redeem men to God. But no more. They will come into this world in a great future display of glory, but they will come to accompany Him.

From the Psalms

The first chapter of Hebrews quotes several Psalms, where the glory of the Son, in contrast with that of created angelic beings, is expressed by God, well in advance of His coming. God cannot forsake His Word, [19] and so each of these has been destined to come true with complete certainty. The chapter begins by declaring the fact that not one of them has ever been called "My Son" by God the Father. The Son of God is indeed God Himself, part of the very Godhead. His Father made this clear when He addressed Him personally as God ...*to the Son He says, "Your throne, O God, is forever and ever".*[20] He has now been established clearly by God as the heir of all things and all will be subject to Him. [21] Even the angels are to worship Him. [22] This is something totally reserved for the Godhead, as the apostle John found out when he was about to bow down to the angel who was showing him marvellous things to come; he was told, *"Do not do that ... Worship God".* [23] Anything else is idolatry.

The Son will have total authority over all the nations. He will indeed be the King of all other kings. [24] His throne will never come to an end - He will never be replaced. His rule will be fully just and equitable [25] because He Himself has demonstrated that He loves what is right and hates what is wrong. [26] There will be no compromise; never any devious intentions or ulterior motives from Him as world ruler,[27] for the first time in human history.

"My Son"

The relationship between the Father and the Son has always been unique. Jesus said to His Father on the way to Calvary: *"You loved Me before the foundation of the world"* [28.] This is far beyond God's relationship with any angel. He never called any of them *'My Son',* or said to them, *"I will be to him a father, and he shall be to me a son."* [29] *"My Son"* is a term of great endearment and of total satisfaction to God His Father. During Christ's time on earth, twice God called out audibly from heaven with the words, *"This is my beloved Son, in whom I am well pleased. "* It happened at His baptism, as He was committing Himself to fulfil all righteousness in the service He was about to begin,[30] and again as He was committing Himself to go to Jerusalem to complete that work.[31] And when the work of Calvary was over, God raised Him from the dead, never to die again, and so demonstrated by divine power that He was indeed the Son of God.[32] The unique deity of Christ is beyond question.

God was then able to fully exalt Him to His own right hand, the place of all honour and authority, and make Him the supreme King-Priest forever. This is His inheritance. What delight that must have given God as His Father, as He anointed Him (not any others) with *"the oil of gladness more than Your companions."*[33] The words describing God as the everlasting creator[34] are applied to the Son of God in this Hebrews epistle,[35] for He is the one through whom everything was created. His rule shall never end and He will outlast everything He made. He has been given total authority over everything that exists,[36] His Father will subdue all opposition to Him,[37] and He will rule uninterrupted for ever without challenge.[38]

Other sons

However, to honour His Son, His Father is now bringing many sons to glory. They were all sharers in flesh and blood, and so Christ chose to take on their flesh and blood Himself.[39] As a result they can now partake of His divine nature.[40] This is possible because they have been rescued from the Devil's control by the victory of Christ at Calvary.[41] They now belong to the Son, have become His companions, His 'fellows', His brethren. He is the firstborn among them, the greatest of them all.[42] They can also become partakers of a heavenly calling, far beyond what they could aspire to naturally, to become those obedient people among whom God can live together now through the Holy Spirit. And for them, the Son now leads their praise to God in heaven itself.[43]

What a privilege that we have been enabled to become companions of such a vastly superior Messiah-King-Priest. All glory goes to Him and to His God and Father!

References: (1) Phil.2:7 (2) Isa.35:5-6 (3) Matt.11:2-10 (4) Rev.1:7 (5) Phil.2:10 (6) Phil.2:11 (7) Jn 1:41 (8) Matt.28:18 (9) 1 Cor.15:25 (10) Heb.3:5-6; 9:9 (11) Heb.4:8 (12) Heb.10:19,22 (13) Heb.7:11,19 (14) Heb.10:11-14 (15) Heb.12:22 (16) Isa.6:1-2 (17) Matt.11:27 ESV (18) Heb.2:9 (19) 1 Pet.1:23-25 (20) Heb.1:8 (21) Ps.2:8; Heb.1:5 (22) Ps.97:7; Heb.1:6 (23) Rev.22:8-9 (24) 1 Tim.6:15 (25) Ps.93:2; Heb.1:8 (26) Ps.11:7; Heb.1:9 (27) Ps.45:4; Heb.1:8-9 (28) Jn 17:24 (29) Heb.1:5 ESV (30) Matt.3:17 (31) Matt.17:5 (32) Rom.1:4 (33) Heb.1:9 (34) Ps.102:25-27 (35) Heb.1:10-12 (36) Matt.28:18 (37)

Ps.110:1; Heb.1:12 (38) Heb.1:8 (39) Heb.2:14 (40) 2 Pet.1:4 (41) Heb.2:14-15 (42) Rom.8:29; Heb.2:10-11 (43) Heb.2:10-13

Bible quotations from NKJV, unless otherwise stated

JESUS CHRIST: (6) THE HIGH PRIEST - THE SANCTITY OF HIS PRIESTHOOD (JOHN TERRELL)

The subject of the sanctity of the Priesthood of the Lord Jesus is among the most precious and important of all aspects of His character and work. This is not least because it is eternal in its nature. His redemptive work on the cross is past and gloriously completed; His high priestly service is for ever. It is almost as though everything in His experience, reaching into past eternity and culminating in His resurrection, has been preparation for an unending heavenly role in which His redeemed people will share. Amazing as the truth is that then...*His servants shall serve Him.*[1] it is still more amazing that He will eternally continue a priestly service for us, though its precise nature and outworking is not revealed.

As we shall see, His function as High Priest on our behalf today is wonderful and often inadequately appreciated by us. Then, when knowing *just as I also am known,*[2] we can only imagine in eager anticipation, His priestly function in the heavenly realm in eternity. The rite of sanctification to priestly service begins in Scripture with the sanctification - setting apart for holy office - of Aaron and his sons. *You shall...consecrate him, that he may minister to Me as priest.*[3] This was a service to God and to His people Israel, and certain associated principles are referred to in Heb.5:1-4. There we read that the high priests must be of human birth, representing men to God and God to men. They are called and appointed by God, we are told, to offer both gifts and sacrifices for sins. Verse 5 of this chapter reminds us that the Lord Jesus did not glorify Himself to be made a high priest; His office, too, was established by divine appointment. *You are my Son; You are a priest for ever according to the order of Melchizedek.* The comparisons

26

between the Aaronic priesthood and that of Christ are themselves instructive both as to appointment and function, but the contrasts are even greater, as we shall see.

The process of setting apart, or sanctifying, for priestly service of the family of Aaron started inevitably with sinful, failing men. Hence their need to offer sacrifices for their own sins before they could stand between men and God and offer on behalf of others. Their sanctification was essentially ritual and ceremonial in nature, though personal holiness was also required. When we come to think of the preparation for, and sanctification of, the Lord Jesus as our High Priest in New Covenant context, we are impressed with the vastness of the superiority of the Lord's high office. The anticipation of His priestly office on behalf of a redeemed people today goes back into eternity.

Then we read in Jn 10:36 of the Lord Jesus as *Him whom the Father sanctified and sent into the world.* This sanctification was for the whole work of salvation, not only in the Lord's earthly ministry in *the days of His flesh;* not only in the accomplishment of His suffering and His ultimate atoning death on the cross; but also in all that flowed to God's glory and our eternal joy in His triumphant resurrection. Heb.5:5-10 fills this truth out for us, showing that the proclamation of His eternal Melchizedek-like priesthood has a special association with resurrection, expressing perfect divine satisfaction in the work of eternal salvation. And we read of the Lord *learning obedience by the things which He suffered.* The unique priestly ministry of Melchizedek as mentioned in Gen.14 is something which could be further considered with profit in relation to the Lord Jesus (see Heb.7), but space does not permit this now. Its eternal dimension is, however, an outstanding feature as we have seen.

Now temptation was a most important element of the Lord's suffering as recounted in Lk.4. There we read that He *was filled with the Holy*

Spirit and *led by the Spirit,* having already been anointed by the Spirit in His baptism at the Jordan. Having emerged triumphant from the wilderness temptation, He *returned in the power of the Spirit to Galilee.*[4] From all of this we can see the work of the Holy Spirit in the Lord's sanctification and preparation for High Priestly work. In Heb.4:14-16 we are reminded very preciously that the One who stands for us before the throne of grace enables us to come there *with boldness* in search of divine mercy and grace. And sometimes we need the very special help of the Holy Spirit in our prayers.[5]

Finally, since our study has its main focus on the sanctity and sanctification of our great High Priest, we must note also that He sanctified Himself.[6] The wonderful prayer of Jn 17 has often been referred to as the Lord's high priestly prayer. Its content, which expresses concern for *those whom You have given Me,* and again, for *those who will believe in Me through their word,*[7] justifies the description of this prayer as high priestly though the Lord only entered on that lofty role in resurrection glory.[8] Thus, we see the total commitment of the Godhead to this glorious office of high priest extending forward for our endless blessing into the great eternal 'forever'.

Turning to the content of the Lord's high priestly service for His people today, we remind ourselves of the role as a dual one; representing men to God and God to men. With regard to the former we have already made reference to Heb.4:14-16 and reflected briefly on the wonder of a divine High Priest who can *sympathize with our weaknesses* and was *tempted as we are, yet without sin. Let us therefore come boldly to the throne of grace.* To Him and through Him we come with all that expresses our need for mercy and grace. But we do not only bring our petitions and prayers through Him and receive that blessed outflow of mercy, grace and forgiveness; we also place into the hands of our High Priest our adoration, thanksgiving and worship such that He offers these as gifts. Nor does He, like the priests of Israel, have to offer sacrifices for sins. Israel's priests were erring men, while our High Priest is the glorious sin-bearer of Calvary whose hands are wholly taken up with offering gifts. The only sacrifice He offers is our sacrifice of praise, because in respect to sins He has already offered one sacrifice for ever.[9]

In representing God to us our great Priest is supremely qualified through His perfect humanity, in all its purity, to graciously mediate the mercy and grace of God; the joy and assurance of His own divine presence as we feed on Him in the Word and in communion. Paul assures the Ephesian disciples that we are blessed with every spiritual blessing in the heavenly places in Christ.[10] Is not the heavenly throne of grace one of those heavenly places? We are not staying now to write of the very special access of the people of God in collective worship into the holies [11] where also the Great Priest over the house of God mediates and serves our privileged presence in collective worship in heaven. Of this more will be written in a subsequent article in this series.

References: (1) Rev.22:3 (2) 1 Cor.13:12 (3) Ex.40:13 (4) Lk.4:14 (5) Rom.8:26 (6) Jn 17:19 (7) Jn 17:9,20 (8) Heb.8:4 (9) Heb.10:12 (10) Eph.1:3 (11) Heb.10:19-25

Bible quotations from NKJV

JESUS CHRIST: (7) THE MEDIATOR: THE SUPERIORITY OF THE NEW COVENANT (DAVID VILES)

"Could do better..."

Perhaps this phrase evokes uncomfortable memories from our school days, recalling room for improvement in matters sporting or academic. In the matter of divine covenants, however - the arrangements established by God to regulate His relationship with the human race -there could never be any need for improvement: *his works are perfect, and all his ways are just.*[1] Nevertheless, we are assured more than once in the letter to the Hebrews that God - who Himself established the "old' Covenant mediated by Moses with Israel - came to judge the law of that covenant to be very less than perfect, in fact weak and unprofitable.[2]

The problem was not with God, whose foreknowledge envisioned the defects of the Old Covenant and provided for their rectification, but with the people of Israel and their failure to live up to their side of the arrangement, despite their initial enthusiasm - *"All that the LORD has said we will do."*[3] God could, and would, do better - through the New Covenant.

The context

The question must therefore be asked, why did God take such infinite pains to uphold His Old Covenant with such a *rebellious and stiff-necked* people?[4] While we cannot presume to question the dictates of God's sovereign will, we are told that the Old Covenant was a temporary arrangement with a national focus. Its implications brought both glory and ultimate disaster (through disobedience) to the Israelite nation, but in God's ongoing purpose it was merely a stage - a *tutor to bring us to Christ, that we might be justified by faith.* [5] In God's eternal plan, this narrow national focus was to be replaced with New Covenant blessings lavishly bestowed on all those (Jew and Gentile) so justified, under a covenant mediated by none other than Christ Himself.

Such an extension of God's purposes was challenging for Christians of Jewish descent, steeped in the nationalistic context of a glorious covenant which God declared nevertheless to be obsolete and ageing.[6] The temptation, particularly under the prevailing persecution,[7] to reintroduce a 'Jewish' gloss to their new lives in Christ, or even to revert to the security of Old Covenant practices, was strong and pervasive. It earned consistent opposition and a stinging rebuke from the Apostle Paul who had himself made the same spiritual journey to Christ - *how is it that you are turning back to those weak and miserable principles ... to be enslaved by them all over again.*[8]

By divine inspiration, the writer of the Hebrews epistle takes a less confrontational approach. We are privileged to be led by him into a presentation, in exalted and explicit detail, of the flawless facets of the New Covenant;[9] like a precious jewel, he scrutinises it closely in comparison and contrast with the limitations of the Old. Glorious and exalted the Old Covenant undoubtedly was both in its inception and application, but, as Paul insisted, its glory is far eclipsed by that of the New Covenant because through it God did *better* - the characteristic word of the Hebrews letter.

Better ... best

In fact, we are confronted, not just with the comparative, but with the superlative. It is not only that the New Covenant is 'better' than the Old - it is 'perfect' (fulfilled, complete) because it is focused on a perfect High Priest, the Son of God.[10] As he makes clear at the beginning of his argument, the writer has much to say about the priesthood of Christ.[11] In a passage which must have left its original Jewish readers stunned by its Spirit-driven audacity, the writer emphasises that the claims of the Lord Jesus to high priestly status, so specially identified with, and reserved to, the descendants of Aaron in the Jewish mind, predated and surpassed the appointment even of Aaron himself.[12]

A companion article in the previous issue of NT examined the superiority of the high priesthood of Christ in the royal order of Melchizedek. Suffice it to note here that Hebrews lays particular stress on the centrality of the divinely ordained priesthood to the nature of the covenant - *when there is a change of the priesthood, there must also be a change of the law;*[13] the imperative is clear - a new priesthood means a new covenant. Centuries before, Korah and others had dared to aspire to the priesthood, rebelling against the authority of Moses and Aaron. Their punishment from God was as sudden as it was exemplary and it entered into the annals of Israel - *that no outsider, who is not a descendent of Aaron, should come near to offer incense before the Lord.*[14] So there was neither a change in the priesthood nor (therefore) a change in the covenant at that time. The Hebrews epistle confirms that it is for no-one (not even the Son of God) to assume the position of priest for himself. God alone must ordain who is to be accorded this signal honour as He had done with Aaron and his sons,[15] and God chose His Son to fulfil this New Covenant role - as a priest in the ancient Melchizedek order, not descended from mortal Aaron, but possessing indissoluble life.[16]

Emphasising the importance of this change of priesthood and differentiating it sharply from what went before at Sinai, our writer is inspired to refer to two verses from the Psalms - short, but full of significance for the authority of our great High Priest. The first emphasises the Lord Jesus' fitness for this exalted office, as the eternally begotten Son of the Father.[17] The second, repeated later in the epistle, stresses that His appointment was made on the basis of an irrevocable oath spoken by God Himself.[18] It is most unusual for Scripture to refer to God in a way which links the finality and permanence attached (humanly speaking) to an oath[19] with the awesome nature of a divinely sworn statement, but such is the import of these verses. We are solemnised by what is being stated - God is binding Himself finally and permanently to the appointment of His Son as High Priest and, therefore, to the terms of the New Covenant of which He is the focus. As a result of this oath, His High Priest offers us "gilt-edged collateral' - a full guarantee (surety) of the benefits of the New- Covenant, because Christ is Himself that surety.[20]

The privileges of the New Covenant

With such a High Priest, such a Mediator, such a Surety, how can the New Covenant fail to be far 'better' for its beneficiaries than what went before? Human failure undermined the benefits of the Old, but the Lord Himself assures us that the New Covenant is founded upon His blood *shed for many for the remission of sins.*[21] Nothing, not even human failure, can detract from the merits of that blood – it 'speaks for us before [God's] throne, proclaims redemption's work is done.'[22] *For this reason*[23] – the authority of His own shed blood - Christ is the Mediator of the New Covenant.

This better sacrifice engenders 'better promises' for the believer than were available under the Old Covenant. Hebrews redefines a striking prophecy of Jeremiah's - which will be applicable also to redeemed Israel in a future day - applying it to the foundational promises of the New Covenant: God's will inculcated in human hearts by the indwelling Spirit rather than imposed by external commandment, with the crowning assurance of God not only forgiving but forgetting our sins[24] and the guarantee (from the Mediator of the covenant Himself) *of the promised eternal inheritance.*[25]

The intimacy with God implied by these better promises anticipates the most precious of the 'better things' identified in the epistle - *a better hope, through which we draw near to God.*[26] Under the Old Covenant, that high privilege of access into God's most holy presence was available only once a year and only then through the representative high priest. In contrast, our hearts thrill to the divine invitation to draw near, with confidence, in worship - *in full assurance of faith* through the merits of that shed blood.[27] Do we value this enormous opportunity as we should? To be welcomed into God's own sanctuary - a place of joy where we meet God and the Mediator Himself; the writer can only use terms which were precious to his hearers - Mount Zion, the heavenly Jerusalem[28] - to attempt to describe this place, the glory of which transcends our understanding. In telling contrast is the fearful and terrible meeting place of Sinai, where a holy God initiated the Old Covenant relationship, glorious as it was![29] Through the Mediator of the New Covenant, our access is very far *better* - in fact, *perfect.*

References: (1) Deut.32:4 NIV (2) Heb.7:18 (3) Ex.24:7 (4) Deut.31:27 NIV (5) Gal.3:24 (6) Heb.8:13 (7) Heb.12:3-7 (8) Gal.4:9 NIV (9) 2 Cor.3:7-11 (10) Heb.7:11 (11) Heb.5:11 (12) Heb.7:1-16 (13) Heb.7:12 NIV (14) Num.16:40 (15) Ex.28:1; Heb.5:4-5 (16) Heb.7:16 (17) Ps.2:7; Heb.5:5 (18) Ps.110:4; Heb.5:6; 7:20-21,28 (19) Cf. Heb.6:16-17 (20) Heb.7:22 (21) Matt.26:28 (22) J.B. Belton

- O Lord Thy courts we humbly tread, PHSS 99 (23) Heb.9:15 (24) Heb.8:8-12 (25) Heb.9:15 NIV (26) Heb.7:19 (27) Heb.10:19-23 (28) Heb.12:22-24 (29) Heb.12:18-21

All Bible references from NKJV, unless stated otherwise

JESUS CHRIST: (8) THE FORERUNNER - THE SUBSTANCE OF THE TRUE TABERNACLE (BRIAN FULLARTON)

To understand the meaning of the word *forerunner* in Heb.6:20, we have to bear in mind that the Lord Jesus always in His earthly life had the thought of a future day before Him, following His perfect sacrifice and preparation for His unique high priestly activity, when an expectant and eager people (the 'us' of verse 20) would be in readiness to do service to God in spiritual worship, having firmly laid hold of 'the hope' set before them (v. 18). This surely has to do with the collective approach of a people to God in His sanctuary, dependent, as was Israel in the past, on the pre-entrance of their high priest into the most holy place (also called *the Holiest of All[1]*) in the earthly sanctuary, but with two major differences:

(1) Israel's priestly representative alone made his way into the most holy part of the tabernacle without any later accompaniment by the people on whose behalf he was acting;[2] moreover, he was only there for a very limited time.

(2) The purpose of Aaron's entrance and service, as high priest, on one specific day of the year in Israel's calendar, was to make atonement with the blood of the sin offering, first for himself and then for God's people, whom he was representing.

In the case of the Lord Jesus, His entry fully opened the way for His people to follow directly into the very presence of God - the Majesty in the heavens - where He is seated at His Father's right hand.[3] He is there constantly in His Father's presence. When we come in worship, that's where we are; exactly where He is.[4] Then again, He is not in the true tabernacle above to make atonement for our sins; He did that gloriously on the basis of His sacrifice at Calvary. His service is important in leading His people in praise and worship, at which time in that heavenly place He still speaks worthily of the Father to our hearts as we are engaged in meditation and adoration, and joyfully proclaims His Father's glories and attributes in song with perfect pitch and tone.[5]

The Tabernacle: the way of approach to God

When we consider the layout of the Mosaic tabernacle, that magnificent structure of the dwelling place of Almighty God on earth, and in particular the location within it where He would directly communicate with His servant Moses, we can understand the long period of time Moses willingly spent in the mountain in Sinai. He was 'with God' forty days and nights, learning everything that had to be learned- *"According to all that I show you..."* [6]It is unsurprising that such detail is so minutely recorded, for there are so many lessons to be taught from the significance of every item of furniture mentioned. Their existence, focus and purpose is to give us a fuller and greater understanding of the excellencies of the Son of God.

Above all, the inner chamber of God's holy presence was to be the place of the highest privilege and fellowship that could be experienced by an earthly mortal.[7] However, skilfully woven and brilliantly coloured curtains, standing wooden boards with horizontally fixed bars, in addition to the dividing veil between the holy place and the most holy place,[8] ensured that the way of approach was no mere ramble. Each step of the journey in coming to God had to be carefully considered; after all, this was the Lord's own master-plan.

The ritual necessary in coming before God is emphasised in the preparation of the holy garments that had to be worn by the high priest. These garments reflected God's glory and the beautiful service which His chosen representative could undertake.[9] Elaborate touches of jewellery adorned the head and body of the high priest in his daily priestly ministry to God for His nation.[10] Close attention had to be paid to the demanding minutiae of the sacrificial system, all of which pointed forward to that one supreme self-sacrifice of the Son.[11] We can readily imagine on that great Day of Atonement, *Yom Kippur,*[12] the whole camp of Israel would be at a standstill. No person was allowed to go near the tent of meeting. They couldn't see where exactly Aaron was, never mind what he was doing, after he made his way into the first compartment, the Holy Place. Then, after changing into his simple linen garments, he went on through the intervening veil into the holiest of all, all the while serving in silence. No such repetitions are needed today in this age of divine grace.

The all-important passage of Heb.10:19-23

Many Christians today are missing out on the great truth unfolded in the narrative above. The setting for this climax of earthly, but sanctified human activity in divine/heavenly service has to do with the responsibility of brothers and sisters[13] in the house of God, in and over which the Lord Jesus is a great priest.[14] Corporate divine service assumes our coming and being together in churches of God,[15] carrying out the word and will of God, all part of what is described as *the confession of our hope;*[16] that is our assurance and conviction that we are where God wants us to be in testimony for Him, and defending and propagating what He has revealed to us concerning the faith.[17] Unlike the nation of Israel, we ourselves fully enter in to the presence of God in worship, through the veil, that is spoken of as the blood-stained offering of Jesus' body - His flesh - in sacrificial death for us.[18] It is all there for us to grasp and enjoy such a wonderful blood-bought privilege, week by week, for the rest of our earthly lives.

What now?

How sad it would be, if He is there in God's presence - as He most certainly is - waiting for us to come to worship on the first day of the week,[19] and we are not there because of our possible deliberate physical absence. The voice of the worshipper rings out clearly and appealingly:

Praise is awaiting You, O God, in Zion ...[20]

Oh come let us sing to the Lord!

Let us shout joyfully to the Rock of our salvation.

Let us come before His presence with thanksgiving;

Let us shout joyfully to Him with psalms ...

Oh come, let us worship and bow down:

Let us kneel before the Lord our Maker.

For He is our God,

and we are the people of His pasture,

and the sheep of His hand.[21]

We come to the Remembrance to celebrate the Lord's death, eat the Lord's supper, and be at the Lord's table[22] - what a wonderful opportunity is ours!

Bible quotations from NKJV unless otherwise stated.

References: (1) Heb.9:3 (2) Ex.30:10; Heb.9:7 (3) Heb.8:1; 9:24 (4) Heb.10:19-22 (5) Heb.2:12 (6) Ex.25:9 (7) Ex.25:22 (8) Ex.26:1,15,26,33 (9) Ex.28:2 (10) Ex.28:6-43 (11) Ex.29 (12) Lev.16 (13) Heb.10:19 - although the masculine *adelphos* is used the word also has a wider meaning of those who share in a common heritage or origin (14) Heb.10:21 RV (15) Heb.10:25; 1 Cor.11:16-18,20,22; 14:23 (16) Heb.10:23 (17) Jude 1:3; 1 Tim.1:19b; 1 Tim.3:9; 2 Tim.3:8; 2 Tim.4:7 (18) Heb.10:20 (19) Acts 20:7 (20) Ps.65:1a (21) Ps.95:1-2,6-7 (22) 1 Cor.11:20,26; 1 Cor.10:21

FIRE! (GILBERT GRIERSON)

The man was a smoker. Caught in the hospital corridor by the sister of the ward where he was a patient, he hastily looked for somewhere to dispose of his cigarette. Ah, a chute in the wall! In went the cigarette, still smouldering. Down to the basement it fell, into a linen skip. Soon the skip was ablaze. The fire spread upward, out of control. Before long the whole hospital tower block was engulfed in flames and smoke. Desperate staff tried to evacuate helpless patients trapped on the upper storeys. Many sick, frail, elderly patients, the bed-bound and children had no chance to escape. Frightening? The above description is from a film shown some years ago to hospital staff in one part of the UK to alert them to the danger of fire in their work environment.

Fire is to be feared!

Fire in the Scriptures is used to describe the eventual experience of the unsaved. It is the Lord Jesus who will one day say, *"Depart from me, you cursed, into the eternal fire prepared for the devil and his angels."*[1] In Rev.20 the lake of fire is described graphically as being the ultimate, eternal destiny of the Devil. How thankful we should be that as believers we are saved by the grace of our God from eternal fire.

Fire cleanses!

When the Lord Jesus entered the Temple courts in Jerusalem to cleanse God's house of the market traders and money changers,[2] He was, in character, *refiner's fire.*[3] He was eaten up with zeal for the holiness of God's house. It was meant to be a holy place, in keeping with God's nature. Men had defiled it. The Lord Jesus swept them away with divine and yet compassionate majesty, (for He did not overturn the tables on

41

which the doves were sold) and vindicated the holiness of His God and Father.

Fire consumes!

On a wet and windy Sunday morning in Belfast, Northern Ireland, many years ago, an incident happened on the way home from attending church that forever changed the life of a young local girl. Moved by compassion to help a frail old lady carrying a heavy bundle along the street in the wind and rain, and feeling very embarrassed in front of lots of 'respectable' Christians, just as they were passing a drinking fountain at the road-side, some verses of Scripture suddenly flashed into Amy Carmichael's mind: *Gold, silver, precious stones, wood, hay, stubble; every man's work shall be made manifest; for the day shall declare it, because it shall be revealed by fire; and the fire shall try every man's work of what sort it is. If any man's work abide...*[4]

The experience was so real that Amy turned to see who was speaking to her. Recalling the incident, she writes years later, 'I turned to see the voice that spoke with me. The fountain, the muddy street, the people with their politely surprised faces, all this I saw, but saw nothing else. The blinding flash had come and gone; the ordinary was all about us. We went on. I said nothing to anyone, but I knew that something had happened that had changed life's values. Nothing could ever matter again but the things that are eternal.'[5]

Amy Carmichael had realised that at the judgement seat of Christ our works as believers are going to be assessed. Only the works that survive the consuming fire will remain, worthy of being rewarded. Should that not cause each one of us to search our hearts and test the motives for all that we do and to examine our lives to see what we are spending our time doing?

"Only one life, "twill soon be past,

Only what is done for Christ will last.' [6]

Fire shines!

The Lord Jesus described John the Baptist as *a burning and a shining lamp.*[7] Through his preaching, the hearts of many were laid bare and lives were changed. John shone powerfully for God in a sinful and needy generation! How we, too, as believers should long to be rekindled in our love for the living God, and earnestly desire a deeper experience of Him, whose eyes are described in Revelation as being *a flame of fire.*[8]

References: (1) Matt.25:41 (2) Jn 2:13-17 (3) Mal.3:2 (4) 1 Cor.3:12-14, KJV (5) Frank Houghton, Amy Carmichael of Dohnavur (6) C.T. Studd, Only One Life (7) Jn 5:35 (8) Rev.1:14

Bible quotations from ESV unless stated otherwise.

TIME, TALENTS & TRAVEL - AN INTERVIEW WITH KEVIN BEAL, BRANTFORD, CANADA

Would you please share with our readers, Kevin, a little about your background?

At age 5 my parents sent me to a local United Reformed church Sunday school. During this time my father got me to memorize Jn 3:16. I knew the words, but I didn't understand their meaning at that time. My parents took us to several different churches because my father was never happy with what any of them taught. One day he came home and said we were going to attend a church in London, Ontario. It was called the Church of God. My father had attended the Church of God in Brantford, Ontario earlier in his life. He told us he believed it taught the truth and was where we should be attending.

At the Church of God in London I had a great Sunday school teacher by the name of Paul Whitehouse. He taught me what the verse that I had memorized years before meant. I was now 8 years old and I had found out how to be born again. The time came when my parents felt it necessary to transfer to the Church of God in Brantford, Ontario. Over the years I attended Mount Forest camp. Once I reached the age of 14, I was too old to attend as a camper; however, I was still able to go as a dishwasher! It was during this time that I, and the two other dishwashers, decided we wanted to live our lives for the Lord. Soon after camp we were baptized and added to the Church of God in Brantford. My years in Brantford have been of great importance to me. I have been surrounded by great men and women of God. They have helped to shape me into the person I am today.

Where have you travelled to in order to visit and support the work of churches of God?

My travels have taken me to most of the Churches of God. If I was to list them all, it might be easier to list the ones I haven't been to! The places I've spent the most time in over the years would be Colorado, British Columbia, Australia, and the Philippines.

How did the desire to do this come about?

All my life I had dreamed of seeing the Canadian Rocky Mountains. By 1998 I had saved up enough money to make the trip. I decided to visit beautiful British Columbia in August while Camp Discovery was on. This was the first trip I ever took on my own and it was the first sign of the travelling spirit I have today. My desire for camp work led me to Colorado the following summer. One summer after camp, a full-time worker asked me if I had ever thought of going to India. I couldn't stop thinking about it. I emailed him a few weeks after and asked if he was serious. He said yes, and a two month trip to India and Burma was planned. That trip showed me what the life of a 'Lord's Servant' was like. I came home knowing it was important for me to give more of my time to the service of God. My desire to serve God has always been the main reason for my travels.

How do you manage to support yourself financially while you do this regularly?

Before I started to do this regularly I had worked on a farm for 15 years. During those years of farming I gained a lot of experience in many ways. People in my home area know me well and are always looking for me to work for them. Truck-driving is now the main thing I do when it comes to farming. On top of this, I work for myself doing home renovations. I have been blessed with many trade skills and it's easy to find jobs between travels and during my travels. The money I earn is just enough to support myself and pay for my travels.

What do you find especially satisfying about the kind of ministry you are able to assist with?

I get to know people by not just standing up preaching to a group and then leaving. I get involved in people's lives. I can spend time in their homes and work alongside them. I get to know those churches, as I know my home church. I feel like I'm at home when I'm with them. It's people that I come in contact with that satisfy me. Seeing God working in lives keeps me motivated!

You are renowned for your practical skills. How do they come into play in your service?

My practical skills have always kept me employed and have been of great value in God's service as well. I remember an elder in my home church, Fred Marks, telling me that God had blessed me with skilful hands and that I should use them. I try my best to use them for God's things, and in doing so many doors have been opened for me to present the gospel and to invite people to the Church. God has definitely led me into situations because of the skills He has given me. I keep my eyes open to this and I believe this is a way the Spirit leads me.

We note you've paid quite a few visits to the Philippines recently - how do you find the difference in culture, and is there anything we could learn from the folks there?

I'm answering this question while I'm in the Philippines. People here are friendly and take a hold on your heart! I feel I'm surrounded by people who want to know about God. I can step out onto the street and in no time I can be telling someone about the Church of God. God's ways are important to them. They want to know the truth and to be close to God. They get excited about Scripture. They memorize it and hide it in their hearts. Seeing this in them shows me that we all could improve our love for the Word. The Bible isn't just any book! It's true and living and full of things we should be excited about.

What's the trickiest situation you've had to face?

In 2011 I went to Israel, Jordan and Egypt to see where the Bible stories took place. I was in Cairo right in the middle of all the destruction and fighting. I had no contact with the outside world. Knowing that my life could be on the line at any moment, I took comfort in the story of Moses. Ex.13 tells how the Lord delivered the Israelites out of Egypt by the strength of His hand. I relied upon His strength and He delivered me out of that tricky situation. Once back in my home church, I found out that an elder there, Trevor Shaw, had mentioned me in the announcements for prayer. He had even said that if God could deliver the Israelites out of Egypt, He could deliver me too. Trevor's words were full of truth! God was

with me and I was delivered home safely!

What do you think you've gained personally in spiritual terms from serving the Lord like this?

I have learned a lot about sacrifice: giving up time for God, to be of service and to live a holy life. I've learned to let go of the typical worldly things we get so focused on in our lives. Jesus said to go and make disciples. Sacrifice is necessary. During my travels I have been in contact with many who daily devote time to the Word, prayer and evangelism. Seeing them putting God before everything else has encouraged me spiritually to do the same.

UPSIDE DOWN VALUES: THOSE WHO ARE MERCIFUL (CRAIG JONES)

There is a story told of the famous French emperor and military general, Napoleon Bonaparte. Several officers and accomplices were discovered in a plot against him and were subsequently sentenced to death for treason. One of them, General Lajolais, had a 14-year-old daughter who, on hearing of the sentence, managed to find a way to appear before Napoleon himself. She threw herself at his feet, crying almost uncontrollably and said, "Sire, mercy for my father, please!" After hearing who her father was, Napoleon replied, "This is the second time he has been found guilty of an attack against the state. He does not deserve mercy." The girl answered, "Sire, it would not be mercy if he deserved it. I plead for mercy!"

This is a good illustration of what 'mercy' really means - the expression of compassion towards someone guilty of an offence, in such a way as to remove the punishment usually required. Simply put, it's the offender not getting what he deserves! When we think about mercy in the context of the Beatitudes of Matt.5 and their wide scope of applicability amongst all people,[1] it's clear that the aspect of 'compassion' included in biblical mercy is what the Lord is drawing attention to as being an admirable characteristic. On a simple level, in situations that can arise in everyday life, it might be seen in giving someone the benefit of the doubt. Perhaps you might hear something negative about someone you know, which seems inconsistent with their character - giving them the benefit of the doubt and not thinking the worst of them would be showing mercy, compassion.

You might have reason to doubt the motivation behind another person's actions towards you or someone else - giving them the benefit of the doubt would be the merciful and compassionate thing to do. Unfortunately, we have a human tendency to want to believe the worst about people, to jump to negative conclusions about them, or the circumstances of the situation they may find themselves in or the motivations for the way they behave. Being merciful means we think more positively about other people.

Of course, it also applies in situations where we have been sinned against, where we have been hurt by someone else physically or emotionally. Instead of retaining bitterness and anger towards the person, we should show a merciful attitude toward them, which, hopefully (if it's not already evident), will bring about a feeling of true sorrow and regret on their part. If they have committed criminal offences, they may continue to face whatever penalty the law imposes, but that does not prevent us granting personal forgiveness, moved by compassion.

This 'beautiful attitude' of mercy is expressed in several different ways in the Bible, which affect the way we should be in our attitude towards other people. For example, it can be seen in the encouragement to *be at peace with all men;*[2] to have an attitude that doesn't stir up contention and bad feeling, that doesn't reciprocate any bad feeling expressed towards us. The Lord also said, *"In everything, therefore, treat people the same way you want them to treat you."*[3] Paul expressed it like this: *So, as those who have been chosen of God, holy and beloved, put on a heart of compassion, kindness, humility, gentleness and patience; bearing with one another and forgiving each other.*[4]

And that brings to us a vital perspective that, as those *chosen of God,* we need to keep in mind as we try to embrace and express this 'beautiful attitude'. We need to constantly remember that we ourselves are the beneficiaries of the greatest expression of mercy that there has ever been, or ever will be. As sinners before a holy and righteous God, we had no defence, no plea, no excuse and, of ourselves, no way to avoid the deserved punishment.[5] But in a loving demonstration of extravagant mercy, God diverted our punishment to His Son, Jesus Christ, when He died on the cross at Calvary. When we came to understand that, appreciate it and believe it by faith in our hearts, we received the mercy of God.

As the Lord Himself has said, *"I gave you an example that you also should do as I did to you."*[6] One of the best ways we can show mercy to others is by sharing with them the life-changing message that we ourselves have believed, that they too may come to believe in the Lord Jesus and receive God's mercy.

References: (1) see Matt.7:28 (2) Rom.12:18 (3) Matt.7:12 (4) Col.3:12-13 (5) Rom.6:23 (6) Jn 13:15

Bible quotations from NASB

UPSIDE DOWN VALUES: THOSE WHO ARE PURE IN HEART (ANDREW DORRICOTT)

How can we see God when the Bible is clear that no one has seen God at any time?[1] The Bible is also clear about our sinful nature,[2] so how is it possible for us to be pure? While purity speaks of being clean, it is also a word meaning 'free from extraneous matter; simple or homogenous'. God knows our heart. In the days of Noah, God saw that people's hearts were continually evil.[3] David cried out to the Lord, in the grieving of his sin, for God to purify his heart.[4] And in John's Gospel it says that Jesus knew the hearts of everyone.[5] It is at the centre of His plan to change our hearts and to cleanse them from all unrighteousness. Our heart speaks of the innermost driving force of what we do and say,[6] and God is ultimately concerned with the condition of it - not only to the point of salvation, however.

Many Christians, and many non-Christians too, for that matter, want to see God at work; perhaps in the midst of a trial, or when facing a big decision, or when praying on someone's behalf. It can be the case where we feel or see very little from God, and that can be a stumbling block in our faith journey. The issues of life are not always an "all's well that ends well" experience, and the perceived lack of action by God can be difficult to understand and accept. When we seek God's help, or His direction, are we single-minded in our heart towards God, or do we feel as though praying to God is just one of many steps to get the answer? Are we so distracted by other situations, people or 'idols' around us that we are unable to see God at work?

Using a specific trial or decision might not be enough to explain this verse, so let's take the principle of a pure heart in the face of an issue and expand it to our daily lives. In a self-assessment of the things you hold dear in your life, can you say that your heart is 'free from extraneous matter' in your devotion and commitment to God? This really is the heart of the verse: to live a life free from idols (meaning *anything* that distracts our devotion away from God). It is a very hard thing to achieve, but perhaps more troubling is that it's very easy to justify not doing so. For fear of reaction or offence, we can compartmentalise our lives into family, work/school, friends, and ourselves as individuals. We can be slightly different people in these different environments, adapting to the social norms or conventions so that we fit in, or succeed, by the world's definition. We justify it by calling it 'balance'. This seems contrary to Rom.12.[7]

If we are able to live our life with a heart that is single-minded, free from extraneous matter, pure in devotion to God, we will see Him more and more at work in our lives and the lives of those around us. We will be more in tune with His Word and His will. Not only will we better see His direction when we ask, but we will see His direction even before we ask. Seeing God in our lives is as much about seeing and recognising the effect of God in all situations, big and small, as it is seeing Him face to face in that future day. Being pure in heart is not strictly a matter of being clean, but being undivided in our devotion in the depth of our heart toward God. A truly undivided heart will establish, maintain and grow our relationship with God to unknown heights. Set aside all the reasoning and justification for those things that distract you from God and conform you to the world, and God will be visible in mighty ways!

References: (1) Ex.33:20; Jn 1:18; 6:46; 1 Jn 4:12 (2) Rom.3:23; 1 Jn 1:8 (3) Gen.6:5 (4) Ps.51:10 (5) Jn 2:24, *also* Matt.9:4 (6) Matt.12:34 (7) Rom.12:2

UPSIDE DOWN VALUES- THE PEACEMAKERS (ANDY SEDDON)

Is it true that much TV entertainment takes advantage of people not getting on with each other? It could be a reality show or a talent contest. Some of it might be healthy competition, but often it is the arguments and fights which have the public talking afterwards. I suppose these shows would be a little boring if all the characters got on well and were nice to each other! In total contrast to this, Jesus declares: *"Blessed are the peacemakers"*.[1] These are people who actively promote harmony and reconciliation. The New Testament word, 'reconciliation' simply means 'to change'. This would be evident, for example, when enemies change into friends or when anger changes into forgiveness.

Jesus goes on to say that peacemakers shall be called *"sons of God."* Why? It is because children take after their parents, and our heavenly Father is the ultimate peacemaker. There are three things that the Bible shows us to be true about God the peacemaker, and therefore should be true also of those claiming to be His children:

God loves reconciliation

Making peace with sinful, rebellious human beings has been at the centre of God's plan ever since Adam and Eve first became His enemies. A wise woman once said to King David: *"God will not take away life, and he devises means so that the banished one will not remain an outcast."*[2] Reconciliation and restoration are themes at the centre of God's heart. If we have personal faith in Jesus Christ, then we have already experienced for ourselves the peace that God brings. In the words of Paul: *you who once were far off have been brought near by the blood of Christ.*

3

If we enjoy this divine peace, then we too should be active in promoting peace with others, especially with our spiritual family who share our salvation. To tolerate bickering and conflict without taking action is not an option. We are to *seek peace and pursue it.*[4] We are to be *eager to maintain the unity of the Spirit.*[5] We are to *strive for peace with everyone.*[6] These words imply earnest, positive action: 'seek', 'pursue', 'maintain', 'strive'.

God acted first

Reconciliation was God's plan, not ours. This is amazing when we remember that God was the innocent and injured party! The Bible states: *all this is from God.*[7] It was *while we were still sinners, Christ died for us.*[8] If you are like me, then you may be prone to stubbornness! If, in the middle of a conflict with somebody, I think - and I stress the word 'think!' - I'm in the right, then I am less likely to take peace-making steps, because this would inflict a painful blow to my pride! After all, why can't the other person come to me? Well, if I am a true child of God, would I not take the initiative, just as God took the initiative for me?

Disunity harms our spiritual service for God. Jesus commands: *"So if you are offering your gift at the altar and there remember that your brother has something against you ... First be reconciled to your brother, and then come and offer your gift"*? Notice here how I must take the step when I am aware my brother has a problem with me!

God made a phenomenal sacrifice

When we've been hurt, taking steps to be reconciled might feel costly. It may cost time or energy, it may require a change in our attitude and behaviour, and it may even feel humiliating! Consider carefully however the price that God has paid: *while we were enemies we were reconciled to God by the <u>death of his Son</u>.*[10] God's love knows no limits. He gave what was most precious to Him so that we could know divine peace. As we think about this, let us pray for the help of the Holy Spirit to bear *with one another ... forgiving each other; as the Lord has forgiven you...*[11] Only when we practise these 'upside down' teachings of the Lord will we know the happiness of being free children of God.

Bible quotations from ESV

References: (1) Matt.5:9 (2) 2 Sam.14:14 (3) Eph.2:13 (4) 1 Pet.3:11 (5) Eph.4:3 (6) Heb.12:14 (7) 2 Cor.5:18 (8) Rom.5:8 (9) Matt.5:23-24 (10) Rom.5:10 (11) Col.3:13

UPSIDE DOWN VALUES - THOSE WHO ARE PERSECUTED (RICHARD HUTCHINSON)

"Blessed are those who are persecuted for righteousness' sake, for theirs is the kingdom of heaven. Blessed are you when others revile you and persecute you and utter all kinds of evil against you falsely on my account. Rejoice and be glad, for your reward is great in heaven, for so they persecuted the prophets who were before you." [1]

The last of the Beatitudes is for those who are persecuted. It is not a subject that I have much personal experience of, and while I am tempted to insert a sincere " Praise the Lord" in there, I wonder whether that lack of persecution is not a comment on the stand I take for the faith. After all, the Scriptures make it very clear in the New Testament that suffering and persecution were to be expected in the Christian life. *Indeed, all who desire to live a godly life in Christ Jesus **will** be persecuted,* Paul told Timothy,[2] and Peter was just as matter-of-fact in his first epistle: *Beloved, do not be surprised at the fiery trial when it comes upon you to test you, as though something strange were happening to you. But rejoice insofar as you share Christ's sufferings, that you may also rejoice and be glad when his glory is revealed.* [3]

So if I find myself in the position of a comfortable Christian, should I rejoice, or should I be asking myself whether my life is not Godly enough to warrant the persecution which is an inevitable consequence for Paul? Should I be surprised at the *lack* of fiery trials, since that seemed the stranger thing to Peter; concerned that I am not sharing in Christ's sufferings to the degree I should be? The New Testament writers prepared the saints for difficulties as the natural course of things and in doing so they were following on from the teaching of the Lord

Jesus. Not only was the Lord alluding to the suffering to be endured on His account in the Beatitudes, but He was repeatedly explicit in flagging up the reality of following Him. In Jn 15:11, after a glorious description of the close relationship with God available through Him as the true vine, which Jesus said He was describing *"that My joy may be in you and your joy may be full",* He outlines clearly that aligning ourselves with God and abiding in Him would mean separating ourselves from the world, which the world would hate us for, just as it hated the Lord Jesus: *"If they persecuted Me they will also persecute you".*[4]

The very qualification Jesus gives for anyone willing to follow after Him is: *"Let him deny himself and take up his cross daily..."*[5] He wasn't hiding the fact that following after Him would bring sacrifice and suffering along with it. The promise of the Lord for those who suffer for His sake is that *"theirs is the kingdom of heaven"* and *"your reward is great in heaven ".* Persecution is called *a fiery trial* by Peter, and it is the purpose of any test or trial to prove the value of something. The testing of our faith in persecution reaps its rewards. *We rejoice in our sufferings, knowing that suffering produces endurance, and endurance produces character, and character produces hope.*[6] That hope is the hope of glory; the joy of knowing that this world is only a temporary dwelling for us, and *So we do not lose heart ... For this light momentary affliction is preparing for us an eternal weight of glory beyond all comparison.*[7]

With such a rich blessing comes the challenge: - When the apostles were arrested and beaten for their preaching we read they went *rejoicing that they were **counted worthy** to suffer dishonour for the name.*[8] If persecution comes to those who live Godly lives and if I have not been afflicted, what is missing from my life to be counted worthy of sharing in the sufferings of my Lord and Saviour? If we are found worthy to endure trials, the challenge then is to *Count it all joy;*[9] *to joyfully accept*™ whatever shape affliction takes and to be content with[10] the hardships of following the one who endured the cross for us for the joy set before Him. He has set before us a joy that should encourage us through whatever this passing world can throw at us.

Bible quotations from the ESV

References: (1) Matt.5:10-12 (2) 2 Tim.3:12 (3) 1 Pet.4:12-13 (4) Jn 15:20 (5) Lk.9:23 (6) Rom.5:3-4 (7) 2 Cor.4:16-18 (8) Acts 5:41 (9) Jas.1:2 (10) Heb.10:34 (11) 2 Cor.12:10

MARRED CLAY IN THE POTTER'S HAND (GERALDE MAG-USARA)

One of the usual requirements when applying for a job in the Philippines is the need to demonstrate a 'pleasing personality'. In our spiritual employment also we need to strive for a pleasing attitude towards God so as to be rewarded in heaven. But we are just helpless clay,[1] and so "... are no more capable of molding ourselves than the clay; we depend upon God as our potter to make us what we ought to be'.[2] It's true that when we are obedient to His will, this pleases God. Sometimes knowing His will is easy, but applying it is difficult.

In his letter to the Romans, even Paul, an apostle of the Lord, before he thanked God for victory through His sinless servant Jesus Christ, tells us: *... I have the desire to do what is good, but I cannot carry it out... When I want to do good, evil is right there with me.* [3]

After having personally become aware of this, he reminded believers at Corinth, *So if you think you are standing firm, be careful that you don't fall.*[4] This is because, as we say, we are not yet perfect. There have been instances when Satan attacks to pull down men and women of God when they are nearly at the peak of their spiritual performance.

Take David as one of the many examples. He was the man 'after God's heart'. He was a mighty warrior king. He killed thousands of enemies,[5] but he was defeated by a single, hidden sin he committed with Bathsheba.[6] As a consequence, he said his bones wasted away through groaning all day long. God's hand was heavy upon him day and night, and his strength was sapped as in the heat of summer - and he begged God to restore to him the joy of his salvation.[7] That's how serious the power of sin is. It could break a stumbled believer into pieces like glass

59

(or a potter's clay jar). The writer of this article experienced something similar to David. He and his fiancé hid their sin after it marred their lives in that they had failed to wait and enter the marriage bed in purity.[8] But nothing escapes from God's sight. He brought their secret out into His light so that everybody knew of it.

However, He had a purpose in revealing it. How merciful is our God, the sinner-lover, who does not just like to smash the potter's jar such that it cannot be repaired, and must be thrown away like the vessel when it was marred![9] What the potter does is to crush the clay together and return to the wheel to begin the work again until the clay takes on the shape the potter originally intended.[10] *"Can I not do with you as this potter does?" declares the LORD. "Like clay in the hand of the potter, so are you in my hand..."*[11]

Yes, it's a deadly experience: very painful. Sitting watching, while those in the church of God were breaking bread, made obvious the big gap between doing God's will and failing to do it. But it was also God's way of shaping us again, through such biblical church discipline,[12] to turn from evil ways and reform wrong actions.[13] Jeremiah's illustration indicates there's a way back - that's the purpose in excommunication. I experienced personally the deadly feeling of guilt through genuine repentance (acknowledging sin, no longer covering iniquities, but confessing) and then the joyful feeling of being forgiven[14] - both personally and by the church. Restored disciples, whose place from God's house has been forfeited while excommunicated, are each like the returning prodigal of the Lord's great story. It's as though I'm alive again![15]

References: (1) Isa.64:8 (2) The Dake Annotated Reference Bible, p.728 (3) Rom.7:14-21 (4) 1 Cor.10:12 (5) 1 Sam.18:7 (6) 2

Sam.12:1-15 (7) Ps.32:3-4; 51:12 (8) Heb.13:4 (9) Jer.19:11 (10) Jer.18:1-4 (11) Jer.18:6 (12) 1 Cor.5:5 (13) Jer.18:11 (14) Ps.51:11; 32:1-5 (15) Lk.15:32

Bible quotations from NIV

RIOTS IN ENGLAND (PETER HICKLING)

Between 6 and 10 August 2011, several London boroughs and cities across England suffered widespread disorder, which was set off by an initially peaceful demonstration against the shooting of Mark Duggan on 4th August during a police operation designed to prevent black-on-black gun crime. Duggan had a gun with him and was a known drug dealer. However, the demonstration was taken over by criminal elements, who turned to violence, looting and arson, which then spread to other people who would not normally have thought of open theft. People in other areas were incited to riot and steal by mobile phone messages, so there was looting in Birmingham, Wolverhampton and Manchester as well as parts of London. Many small shops selling desirable goods such as TVs were broken into and looted, and families lost everything they had. Readers in the UK may well have seen on TV pictures of buildings going up in flames, reminiscent to older ones of scenes of World War 2.

How can these things happen? First, most of the offenders are young - there has grown up a generation of people who have no properly instructed moral sense; they will do what they can get away with. If other people riot they will do the same. Secondly, in many past disturbances, such as those in the 1980s and 2001 in the North, violence was directed against other ethnic groups or the police. In this case, as the BBC report of 15th September put it 'many of those on the streets were out shopping with a crowbar'; it was simple acquisitiveness, wanting things that they couldn't afford to buy. Burglary, i.e. theft from premises, was the primary crime.

This desire is no new thing, and it's not exclusive to rioters; most of us have to confess that we would like things that we couldn't possibly have

- the houses in the front of Country Life magazine, the expensive cars, the yachts. Yet it is deeply unchristian. The Old Testament says, *You shall not covet* (yearn to possess) *your neighbour's house ...or anything that is your neighbour's.* [1] The Lord Jesus reinforced this when he said to a man who wanted him to divide his inheritance, *"Take care, and be on your guard against all covetousness, for one's life does not consist in the abundance of his possessions."*[2] He followed with the parable about the rich man who said that he would store up his goods and *eat, drink and be merry,* but God said to him, *"Fool! This night your soul is required of you."*[3] I expect that most of the readers of this magazine are law-abiding citizens who would not dream of smashing a shop window and stealing a camera, and wouldn't take their wanting to possess as far as theft, but the Lord linked envy ('a feeling of discontented or resentful longing aroused by someone else's possessions...' OED) with *evil thoughts, sexual immorality, theft, murder, adultery, coveting, wickedness, deceit, sensuality, slander, pride, foolishness.* [4] We must therefore look at ourselves as well as at the rioters.

Can we do anything about them? Obviously, they need individual change at heart; the power of Christ within has changed many lives, but this is not easy to bring about. Many of us are too old and too disconnected from their circumstances for communication to be easy, but the love of Christ can bridge the gap if we can show it.

References: (1)   Ex.20:17   (2)   Lk.12:15   (3)   Lk.12:16-21   (4) Mk.7:21-22

Bible quotations from ESV.

GOING AWAY FROM HOME TO STUDY (GREG NEELY)

Parents

Planning for your children's university or college education should start early in their lives, perhaps for some from a financial perspective and certainly for all from a spiritual and maturity perspective. What is true of any financial resources that may be regularly set aside from early childhood into a fund that accumulates without compromising its purpose, must also be true of the resources of scriptural knowledge and application routinely deposited into the minds of our youth without compromising their purpose. Preparing our young people to leave our homes to go away on their own to obtain additional education must start before they are even in primary school. For parents must be the first and most important teachers in our children's lives. Perhaps Lois and Eunice, Timothy's maternal ancestors, knew that very well![1]

Our role as parents is not to cling to our children, nor to raise them to cling to us; it is not to live our lives and ambitions through them; it is not to make them so dependent upon us that they can never live life apart from our influence. That is to ensure immaturity such that when faced with campus life, with all its temptations and influences (not all bad, but certainly not all appropriate for the disciple of Christ), the unprepared student finds his spiritual foundation cracking and his disciple resolve undermined. Our role as parents is surely to teach our children to ... *discipline [themselves] for the purpose of godliness* [2] so that they can ... *be strong in the Lord, and in the strength of His might. [Putting] on the full armor of God, so that [they] may be able to stand firm against the schemes of the devil.*[3] That must, by definition, demand that we ... *bring them up in the discipline and instruction of the Lord.*[4]

64

No short-cuts here; no passing the responsibility; no blaming Sunday School or the elderhood or their peer group. This is our task as parents - but not as dictators, or task masters, nor protectors at all cost. Experiences of trial by our children who have been given appropriate independence while under our roof and under our guidance can be the greatest teachers for them, bringing about greater spiritual maturity and depth of understanding of the Lord's will.[5] Greater than all the instruction we can give is the power of example. If our children see our commitment to the Lord, to the local church and the Fellowship, shown by always attending church meetings and giving the Lord priority in the use of our time, they will more likely do the same. It goes without saying that children should be taken to church meetings from a very young age - even as babies - so that attendance is a regular habit of life.

Students

If your motivation in getting away from home is more about getting away from family and church influences than it is to get the best education you can at the most appropriate learning institute, you are starting off on a very weak footing! Your parents were not perfect in raising you, but they did their best in the fear of the Lord. Their love is unconditional, no matter what you do - or what they say! Their primary ambition for you is not that you become wealthy, famous or appear on the Dean's honour list. Their deepest desire is that you become the person God expects you to be so that you can do the work God expects you to do. The freedom, independence, lack of accountability, the pressures of your peers who do not love the Lord, the differences of belief of those who do love the Lord will all challenge your character. But you: *Be diligent to present yourself approved to God as a workman who does not need to be ashamed, accurately handling the word of truth.*[6] Choose to be ... *a vessel for honor, sanctified, useful to the Master, prepared for every good work.*[7]

Others in the church

Pray for godly parents to be effective at teaching their children, not only about our common salvation, but that they *contend earnestly for the faith which was once for all handed down to the saints.*[8] Pray for young men and women looking forward to their independence and growth at university or college that they will ... *continue in the things [they] have learned and become convinced of, knowing from whom [they] have learned them ...so that the man of God may be adequate, equipped for every good work.*[9]

References: (1) 2 Tim.1:5; 3:15 (2) 1 Tim.4:7 (3) Eph.6:10-11 (4) Eph.6:4 (5) Jas.1:2-4 (6) 2 Tim.2:15 (7) 2 Tim.2:21 (8) Jude 3 (9) 2 Tim.3:14,17

Bible quotations from NASB

MISSION: GLIMPSE OF ETERNITY FROM LIBERIA (LAWRENCE ONYOKOKO)

Liberia was the first independent country in Africa: it celebrated its 164th Independence Day on 26 July 2011. It is a small country with a population of less than four million. There used to be a church of God in Grand Cess, Grand Kru County, but it ceased in the early '80s. There is now an ongoing work to re-establish churches of God in Liberia. Only two known remaining sisters are left of the former Church of God; others presumably have gone to be with the Lord.

Where are you going?

There is an old biblical story of Hagar fleeing from her mistress. An angel of the Lord met her and asked, *"Where have you come from and where are you going?"* Most people in Liberia have no difficulty with the first part of the question: they can trace their origin to God. But only believers in the Lord Jesus can say for sure that they are going to heaven. I was with an older Christian brother doing house-to-house evangelism early in 2011, when we came to an elderly man who was sitting under a mango tree with his family. During our chat with him, my colleague asked him, "I'm sure you would like to go to heaven, yes?" The Liberian Pa, who had been listening with rapt attention suddenly burst out, "I ain't going nowhere, I'm staying right here." We smiled at his ignorance. He obviously had been taking lessons from the sect which erroneously believes only 144,000 will go to heaven.

It has been said that 'if people are told something often enough, and convincingly enough, they will accept it'. The sect is known for using this tactic. I would encourage young believers especially, to keep away from this sect. The apostle Paul says, *Even if we, or an angel from heaven, should preach to you a gospel contrary to what we have preached to you, he is to be accursed.*[1] It is important to note that Rev.7 finds fulfilment during the Tribulation period. 'After these things,'[2] the 'uncountables' also from the Tribulation, will stand before the Lamb and the throne.[3] There is nothing to indicate, as the sect assumes, that it is only the 144,000 who will be in heaven or that only those 'uncountables' will inherit the earth.

The coming to the air for His saints

Although the word 'rapture' (meaning 'transport to heaven') is not expressly written in Scripture, it is implied. Paul speaks of that momentous day when there will be an upward release for believers. The Lord Himself shall descend from heaven and take His own to be with Him.[4] What effect should this have on the believer? The awareness of the Lord's return should encourage the believer to maintain purity of life;[5] perseverance in difficulties;[6] and to preach the gospel.[7] We all have the potential to influence people in a positive way. Nobody is a 'nobody'. There is a saying here, "If you think you are too small to make an impact, try going to bed with a mosquito in the room!"

The coming to the earth with His saints

The Scripture calendar shows approximately seven years between the Lord's coming to the air and then to the earth.[8] The Lord will come to earth with his saints in judgement at the end of the tribulation period and thereafter will set up his millennial reign.[9] The earth will eventually be 'dissolved' and a new heaven and a new earth put in place.[10] As you take a glimpse into the future, can you say for sure where you are going? I will say to the likes of our Liberian friend, 'If you ain't going nowhere, I am going somewhere'. An old chorus says,

I am going higher, yes I am.

I am going higher some day.

I am going above the shadows, into the presence of God.

References: (1) Gal.1:8 (2) Rev.7:9,14 (3) Rev.7:15 (4) 1 Thess.4:16-17 (5)1 Jn 3:3 (6) Rom.8:18 (7) 2 Cor.5:10,11 (8) see Dan.9:24-27 (9)1 Thess.3:13; 2 Thess.1:10; Rev.20:2-10 (10) 2 Pet.3:7-10,13

Bible quotations from NASB

ETHICAL DILEMMAS: (1) CONTRACEPTION (GARETH ANDREWS)

Opinions on the ethics or morality of contraception vary widely in the world today. While some would hold that any form of contraception is biblically prohibited or some believe that any form of artificial contraception is itself 'intrinsically evil',[1] some other people hold those who promote these faith-based views as indirectly responsible for the deaths of millions through 'allowing' the transmission of sexually-transmitted diseases like HIV / Aids.[2] Historically, it seems that people have always held differing views on the use of contraception. However, for many of those who would describe themselves as 'new atheists' or 'humanists', it has undoubtedly in recent years become a focus in the apparent struggle between science / rationalism and religion. Christians today must guard against prevailing attitudes in society either consciously or subconsciously causing us to lower our standards, and we must of course ensure that our opinions are derived from biblical teaching in order to stand up to challenges and assaults that we may face.[3]

The scope of this article looks at the possible use of contraception for a Christian couple within marriage as we clearly learn from the Bible that sexual intercourse outside marriage is wrong.[4] Some Christians may believe that any form of contraception whether natural or artificial is wrong, viewing sexual intercourse as exclusively for the purpose of procreation and receiving the blessing of children.[5] Children are indeed a blessing, among many blessings that are offered to us from our loving God. Through the discussion of temporary abstinence, 1 Cor.7:1-6 teaches us that there is more to sexual intercourse than procreation - is it not also the highest expression of intimacy, love and unity within marriage?[6]

Many Christians see these verses as justifying a natural method of contraception in limiting intercourse to the infertile portion of the wife's monthly cycle. While imperfect like all methods of contraception other than abstinence, this has been used throughout history in attempts to plan families naturally - for various reasons, including allowing newly married couples to get used to their life together or through other motives of responsible parenthood. Other Christians may have concerns over the unreliability or limitations of this natural method and see no biblical difference between natural and most artificial methods of contraception, drawing a parallel to the use of mechanical techniques and chemical treatments widely acceptable in other fields of medicine and healthcare. According to the UK's National Health Service (NHS) there are now around fourteen methods of artificial contraception, with new alternatives and technologies in development. These different concepts vary greatly in the level of protection they offer in terms of the risk of pregnancy and infection, as well as cost, reliability and the potential for damaging side effects. Forms of sterilisation are irreversible and would need to be carefully considered by a married couple on medical advice.

What about the concept of 'emergency contraception' such as the 'morning-after pill'? Through its possible action of preventing the implantation of a fertilised ovum, rather than preventing conception itself, this might better be described as a form of abortion rather than contraception. The issue of abortion will be explored in a subsequent article in this series. With 1 Cor.6:19-20 as a guide, we should seek to avoid any practice that is harmful to our bodies. Christians should be guided by factual information and medical advice, but also by individual exercise of conscience. We must also be aware that the very consideration of the potential or merits of parenthood itself can be highly emotive raising questions of unity, selfishness or responsibility that couples may wish to discuss and prayerfully consider before and during marriage.

References: (1) Vademecum for Confessors concerning some aspects of the Morality of Conjugal Life, Pontifical Council for the Family, February 12, 1997 (2) Austen Ivereigh, Catholics, Condoms and Africa, The Guardian, June 26, 2004 (Religion) & April 8, 2005 (Politics) (3) Rom.12:2 (4) 1 Cor.6:18-20; Heb.13:4 (5) Ps.127:3-5 (6) Gen.2:24

ETHICAL DILEMMAS: (2) ASSISTED REPRODUCTIVE TECHNOLOGIES (DR. JOHN ROBINSON)

Ethics discussions often lead to intense and unexpected emotional reactions, especially when the topic is reproduction. 'Barren' is a biblical word. Times change and so does the language. Today we speak of 'infertility'. It is a softer way to describe a sad and stressful problem for many married couples. Although God commanded both Adam and Eve, and later Noah, to be *fruitful and multiply*[1] this was appropriate in the context of God's new creation. A child is not something owed to one, but a marvellous gift from God.[2]

Ps.139 talks about God's infinite care over our creation, while Rom.8:22 refers to the 'groaning' of creation. We spend our lives trying to reconcile the beauty of it all with the pain resulting from the mystery, flaws and incompleteness of the creation we know now. Most find ways to cope; for others it can be too much to bear. Medical treatment for infertility became available almost 100 years ago with the introduction of artificial insemination. *In Vivo* Fertilisation is where male sperm is inserted into the female. Specific drugs are usually needed for this method. Attempts were later made outside the body, in a 'test tube'. It was not until 1960 that IVF *(In Vitro* Fertilisation) became widely available. The successful birth of Louise Brown in England (a 'test tube' baby) in 1978 heralded a new era in the treatment of infertility.

Infertility has been the source of great sadness and even anguish for some married couples, even in Old Testament times. There were Rebekah, Sarah, Hannah, Manoah's wife and Elizabeth.[3] God did intervene with these particular women and prayer was a big factor. God has granted the knowledge and ability to doctors and biologists to develop technologies to treat and help many medical conditions. Science has made the improbable, the implausible, and often the 'impossible', come true: for example, pacemakers for hearts; transplants of different organs; corrective surgery for deformities - and IVF.

The attitude to assisted reproductive technologies (ART) varies amongst Christian and cultural groups (e.g. ART is not accepted by the Vatican.) The churches of God - along with Jewish and Islamic people - accept ART, but (a) only between married couples, (b) a third party donor is unacceptable, (c) surrogate motherhood is not accepted, and (d) there must be no embryo wastage. Within these constraints there is conformity to the design for the generation of families which the Scriptures consistently expect. From a Christian point of view, we accept the conclusions above, for the following reasons:

(a) Each individual begins with fertilization, and is a unique creation with a special worth to God, whom God intends to be conceived within the marriage relationship, sharing not only the love which its parents can give, but also their individual genetic contribution. The concept of the family, where the parents are committed to each other in the sight of God, pervades the Scriptures.

(b) For these reasons, a woman having a child which is biologically someone else's, even if desired and loved, introduces a sort of artificial adultery, where someone else's personality is involved. (Of course, adoption of a child from someone else is accepted).

Children, being a gift from God, are a responsibility from God to the family. Christian couples must pray together and ask God for wisdom.[4] They should also seek godly counsel. Some married couples feel uncomfortable that ART dissociates the sexual act from the procreative act, entrusting the life of the embryo to the scientists. ART is not for every married couple, even if they can afford it. Paul went beyond recommending life without children when advocating a celibate life without marriage[5] so that one could devote more time to accomplishing Christ's command to spread the Gospel message.[6]

The miracle of human life is that we have each been made to be in relationship with God. Relationships take us beyond mere biology. Relationships are used in the New Testament to describe God's own inner life.[7] Relationships are the energy of Christian community: each disciple with Christ, and every disciple one with another.

References: (1) Gen.1:28; 9:1,7 (2) Ps.127:3-5; 128:3 (3) Gen.25:21; 11:30; 1 Sam.2:5; Judg.13:9; Lk.1:7 (4) Jas.1:5 (5) 1 Cor.7:7-8 (6) Matt.28:19 & see Canadian Medical Dental Society, Vol. 31 Issue 1, 2011 (7) Jn 17:21

ETHICAL DILEMMAS: (3) ABORTION (TREVOR SHAW)

A short time ago, I planted a seed. Eventually a green shoot appeared, which grew daily with buds forming along the way, followed by leaves and petals until eventually the flower was in full bloom. When did the life of that flower begin? Only at full bloom; when the buds became apparent; as the shoot emerged or when the first roots emerged from the seed?

Emotions run high on both sides of the abortion debate and many passionately defend their perspectives. What does the Bible say about the issue of abortion (the deliberate artificial termination of an embryonic human or human foetus as it develops from conception to birth)? If we are looking for specific direction in the Bible that says whether or not it is right to have an abortion then we won't find it. However, there are some guiding scriptural principles that can be applied as we explore this subject.

"You shall not murder." [1] Many would assert that to perform an abortion is to take a human life,[2] so the question of when the Bible indicates human life begins is a key component of understanding whether or not abortion is an option for the Christian. Some reason that life as a human being begins when a newborn baby takes its first breath. They refer to God breathing *the breath of life* into Adam[3] to support their perspective, reasoning human life begins outside the womb and therefore conclude abortion is not the same as killing a human being. One problem with this line of reasoning though is Adam was not 'born'. He never grew in a mother's womb and there was no human life before God placed him on the earth as a fully developed human being, so God did something unique to give life to Adam.

Most Christians point to scriptures like Ps.139:13-16, which describes the intricate development of a baby in the womb, to reason that a life begins before a new-born baby takes a first breath. Technology shows the detailed typical week-by-week development of an unborn child: when the brain starts to form; the heart beats; when arms, legs, fingers and toes form; when the baby recognizes sounds and starts to practise breathing. Most mothers sense this growth, especially as an arm or leg stretches or the baby moves position or even hiccups within its mother's womb and many mothers know their baby's personality even before birth! John the Baptist leapt upon hearing the voice of Mary, the mother of the Lord Jesus;[4] Jacob and Esau fought within Rebekah's womb.[5]

In these specific instances both actions indicated the personalities and adult lives those in the wombs would lead. It is also interesting to note the unborn John the Baptist that leapt inside Elisabeth's womb was referred to as a babe ('brephos' in Greek); the born Lord Jesus in the manger in Bethlehem was also referred to as a babe (brephos) [6] as were the young children who were brought to the Lord to bless.[7] Luke describes unborn, newly born and child using the same word, without clarifying whether he is referring to just their physical stage of development or other aspects too. Can we conclude therefore that since all three stages use a consistent word, they are in fact all living people? For many Christians the answer is yes, and based on all these facts they find it impossible to come to any other conclusion than life begins at conception and that to abort a pregnancy is in fact to kill a life.

Perhaps two reasons for the strong opinions on both sides of the debate are the sheer magnitude of the issue and the reasons for abortion. Statistics indicate in the UK and North America, over 20% of all pregnancies are aborted.[8] With availability of technology where the foetus gender can be established, even having an abortion because the unborn child is the 'wrong' gender is becoming more common. However, not every abortion performed is the result of self-centred circumstances. Facts suggest 7% of abortions are undertaken on medical recommendation due to extreme pregnancy health complications in either baby or mother or because the pregnancy was the result of a rape.[9] All these cases must involve extreme anguish for those involved - anguish few of us can ever enter into or understand. As such, and in the absence of explicit scriptural direction, these decisions must be brought before the Lord in all prayerful sincerity, seeking His will and then acting upon it according to one's conscience.

References: (1) Ex.20:13 (2) Ex.21:23 where 'life for life' applies to miscarried foetus (3) Gen.2:7 (4) Lk.1:41 (5) Gen.25:22-23 (6) Lk.2:12 (7) Lk.18:15-16 (8) www.johnstonsarchive.net/policy/ abortion/index.html#CA [1] (9) www. abortionno.org/Resources/ fastfacts.html[2] (cited for statistical reference only, opinions expressed on this website are not necessarily shared by NT)

---

1. http://www.johnstonsarchive.net/policy/abortion/index.html#CA

2. http://abortionno.org/Resources/fastfacts.html

ETHICAL DILEMMAS: (4) EUTHANASIA (BEN JONES)

What would our response be if we were asked to help someone to die? Euthanasia, meaning 'good death', is a result of the idea that there may come a time when death is preferable to continued life, with various arguments being put forward in favour or in defence of the act. However, for a Christian believer, scriptural guidance must be at the forefront of our consideration if ever we are in the situation, or if, more likely, the question is posed to us as a challenge. The intent here, of course, is not to give a definitive answer, because it is almost always possible to come up with 'what if...'" scenarios that challenge ideas about euthanasia. Instead, it is worth considering the implications of our life of service for God whether clearly seen or beyond our immediate perspective.

The topic of euthanasia logically leads us to consider the question: what are we here on earth to do? To enjoy our life, in any degree, or to glorify God? Although these are not mutually exclusive options, when we truly appreciate the latter, then the former becomes irrelevant. To quote the apostle Paul, *More than that, I count all things to be loss in view of the surpassing value of knowing Christ Jesus my Lord, for whom I have suffered the loss of all things, and count them but rubbish so that I may gain Christ.*[1] In Paul's mind, he considered all other things, notwithstanding any pain or discomfort, as rubbish compared with knowing Christ. In Phil.1:21, Paul states, *For to me, to live is Christ -* declaring that his continued life was valuable because it meant that he was able to serve his Master. For a believer in the Lord Jesus, death is preferable to life in many ways, because death will instantly deliver us into the presence of our Saviour -a much better place to be than here on earth!

Nevertheless, the many commands in the New Testament for the way in which we should serve the Lord demand that we have a life of service ahead of us, however much we may want to be with Him. Advocates of euthanasia often approach the matter from a desire to be compassionate: to relieve the suffering of those for whom there is no reasonable hope of recovery. In a medical situation, there may well be cases where intolerable pain or permanent disability lead to a patient, or family members -or doctors for that matter - considering euthanasia as a compassionate way of easing the pain and discomfort that a loved one is feeling. From the perspective of our loving heavenly Father, seeing one of His children in pain must be a heart-breaking thing, especially since He has power to heal or to 'call home'. Indeed, when the Lord Jesus saw the pain and anguish of His friends over the death of Lazarus, He was moved to tears, even while knowing of Lazarus's imminent resurrection.[2] Compassionate euthanasia may seem like something a loving God would allow or even advocate, and yet the scriptural perspective that *to live is Christ* is something that cannot be ignored.

As followers of the Lord Jesus, it is our purpose, and should be our desire, to glorify Him in all we do and, by the work of the Spirit, the Lord can often be glorified by us without our knowledge. In 1 Kgs.19:18, God reveals to a dejected and defeated Elijah that there were 7,000 people in Israel who remained faithful - an example and testament that God's plans and God's workings are often far beyond what we can see or imagine. Similarly, for someone dealing with incurable pain or disability it may be difficult to see how God can work in the situation to His glory, but we must be aware of how limited our own vision is.

Richard Bach, the author *of Jonathan Livingstone Seagull,* states the guiding principle of a life of service quite succinctly: "Here is a test to find whether your mission on earth is finished. If you're still alive, it isn't!" God has already numbered the days of our lives[3] and has allotted to us works of service[4] - works that we may accomplish even when we feel at our lowest, through the magnificent working of the Spirit. While easier said than done, our life should be constantly focused on serving our Master.

Bearing in mind that God is the author of life, and has the sole right to determine the length of a human life,[5] and that the Bible teaches the sanctity of human life,[6] the Churches of God regard (active) euthanasia as an excommunicable offence; but the termination of 'life support' in 'brain death' cases is regarded as being subject to the exercise of personal conscience based on factual information by those concerned.

References: (1) Phil.3:8 NASB (2) Jn 11:35 (3) Ps.139:16 (4) Eph.2:10 (5) Acts 17:25 (6) Ex.20:13

THE FIRST KISS: GILBERT GRIERSON, KNOCKNACLOY, N. IRELAND

The kiss of the lover

To be in love defies scientific explanation. But romantic love (Greek: *eros*) is something very real. Sometimes it is love at first sight; at other times it develops slowly. However it arises, love is a living thing and is meant to grow, mature and develop. Young lovers may start by holding hands, before the poignant moment when the first kiss is exchanged. What tenderness, over-flowing of affection and oneness of desire is being expressed and exchanged! You can only really know what being in love feels like if you have been in love yourself-like the writer of the 'Song of Songs':

Let him kiss me with the kisses of his mouth!

For your love is better than wine... [1]

It is God who has created the desire for two lovers to kiss each other. Our society is even degrading the romantic kiss, making it part of our throw-away culture where casual relationships with routine kissing are no more than a desire for personal gratification. But for the one who waits for true love, then the kiss has special significance - a bond that two hearts are united in love; a precursor of so many more physical expressions of love, ordained of God, that will naturally follow in time, as that love is consummated within the divinely created framework of marriage. Surely this is something worth waiting for.

The reconciling kiss

Ps.2:12 says: *Kiss the Son, lest he be angry, and you perish in the way, for his wrath is quickly kindled. Blessed are all who take refuge in him.* This unusual verse reminds us that sinners need to be reconciled to God through His Son otherwise they will experience His wrath against sin and suffer the judgement that their sins deserve. This reconciliation is only made possible because *Christ also suffered once for sins, the righteous for the unrighteous, that he might bring us to God.* [2]

Perhaps the coming to Jesus in faith is seen, symbolically, as kissing Him, because it indicates a right relationship has been established with God on a personal level. It is a kiss bringing peace. *Therefore, since we have been justified by faith, we have peace with God through our Lord Jesus Christ.* [3]

The holy kiss

Why did the first Christians greet each other with a holy kiss, probably on the cheek? [4] Was it a sign that the peace and love that had been established between God in heaven and men on earth through the work of the Son was now also being evidenced between followers of Christ on earth? A kiss, something personal, something pure, something that spoke of reconciliation, love and unity, found its expression within the constitution and practices of a new people of God founded upon new covenant truths, expressing the inexpressible and abiding love of God.

The kiss of betrayal

I wonder when was the first time Judas kissed Jesus? In the Garden of Gethsemane it was a kiss indicating treachery in Judas' heart, for he was betraying his Lord and Master. [5] How more corrupt could the meaning of a kiss have become than when it was used as a sign that Jesus was the one whom the armed guards were to arrest and lead away to suffer and die! God was graciously allowing something that was ordained for good (a kiss) to be used by evil to bring about His purposes of love towards those who, by nature, were His enemies.

Conclusion

While some may experience true romantic love on earth, earthly and transient, emotional experiences will be far exceeded by the spiritual realities of heaven when we will be with the One who created human emotions and who is Himself love in all its fullness and completeness. Let us treasure in our hearts that first kiss with the One who loved us and gave Himself for us that we may be for ever with Him, close to His heart.

'Loved with everlasting love, led by grace that love to know;

Spirit, breathing from above, Thou hast taught me it is so.

Oh, this full and perfect peace! Oh, this transport all divine!

In a love which cannot cease, I am His, and He is mine.'[6]

References: (1) Songs 1:2 (2) 1 Pet.3:18 (3) Rom.5:1 (4) 1 Cor.16:20 (5) Lk.22:48 (6) G.W. Robinson

Bible quotations from ESV

SELF-ESTEEM (PAUL MERCHANT)

A large part of life is a kind of endless one-to-one conversation with ourselves. When we are thinking, it's like talking to ourselves, but inside our heads. And in the ups and downs of everyday life, good days and bad days, our thinking gets into repetitive ways of reacting to what happens to us. We use so much intuition and instant interpretation as we react and respond. And when things go wrong that have an impact on us, we often react with thoughts such as, "I never get it right," "I'm not good enough," "Nobody listens to me," "I'm just too tired today," "Oops, failed again," or "Now what will they think of me?" These instant, guilty thoughts often reveal our low self-esteem and, in Christian service, lay on us a burden of failure and of having to earn God's love, to deserve it by working at being successful in His work. How we fail to rest and enjoy the unqualified acceptance, undeserved favour and enduring, abundant love of our God and Saviour!

How do people value themselves by the standards of secular Western society? There are at least three altars at which this society worships, dedicated to the idols of our age - Wealth, Intelligence and Physical Beauty. Many worship these idols by how they use their time, energy, finances and in how they conduct their relationships. Their self-esteem rests precariously on their own assessment of how they satisfy these gods. But these transient, superficial values are not for the Christian. The Christian sees through and beyond and above these hollow gods. The life of Christ displays the true value of people to Himself and to His God.

Jesus' life was full of encounters with people whose minds and hearts He moved from rejection to acceptance, from feeling excluded to being included. The woman at the well was presumably burdened by a life of sin and failure, yet Christ chose to share with her profound truths about worship. This excluded woman with low self-esteem was transformed into the included woman who brought a crowd to see Jesus, *"Come, see a man who told me everything I ever did. Could this be the Christ?"* *They came out of the town and made their way toward him.* 1

Mary brought her expensive ointment to Jesus and she was scorned by the men in Simon's house, but Jesus lifted Mary's damaged self-esteem and publicly applauded her faith, *"When she poured this perfume on my body, she did it to prepare me for burial."*[2] In the Lord's teaching, the prodigal son returned home and his first words to his Father were, *"Father, I have sinned against heaven and against you. I am no longer worthy to be called your son."* But the father's reaction was jubilant talk of the best robe, ring, new sandals, a feast and the fattened calf! [3]

At another banquet prepared for many guests who then gave feeble excuses, the people who were given a warm welcome were, in the end, those who were the lowest in that society - *"Go out quickly into the streets and alleys of the town and bring in the poor, the crippled, the blind and the lame."* [4] How they enjoyed themselves that day, responding to the largesse of their generous host! This is the foundation of the Christian's self-esteem - how God values us. God loved us, chose us, values us and has plans for us!

Not our love, but His - *not that we loved God, but that he loved us and sent his Son as an atoning sacrifice for our sins.*[5]

Not our spirit, but His Spirit, *he has given us of his Spirit.*[6]

Not our life, but His, *Christ loved us and gave himself up for us.*[7]

Our lives do not rely on the daily temperature of our fragile, wavering self-esteem, but on God and our value to Him, *And so we know and rely on the love God has for us.*[8]

References: (1) Jn 4:29-30 (2) Matt.26:12 (3) Lk.15:21-23 (4) Lk.14:21 (5) 1 Jn 4:10 (6) 1 Jn 4:13 (7) Eph.5:2 (8) 1 Jn 4:16

Bible quotations from NIV

PRAYER MAIL - AN INTERVIEW WITH DEREK ADAMS, STOKE, ENGLAND

How did the idea for Prayer Mail first come about?

Several times, during the international Youth Fellowship Rally (YFR) held in 1992 at Kinmel Hall, I stood on the stairs watching lots of people talking while they were in queues at meal times. I wondered over and over again how they would all be able to keep in touch with each other after YFR was over. So, it could be said that the seeds of Prayer Mail started to germinate on the stairs at Kinmel Hall!

Working on the idea for some time led to the development of a feasible plan which was then shared with other young (at the time!) men in the Stoke-on-Trent Church of God and we worked on it together at the church hall.

We designed a matrix of groups where, in each group, a single prayer point would begin to be circulated by post around the group with other prayer points being added to it by group members as it circulated. Eventually, it was forwarded to the leader of another group who would then begin its circulation around that group, and so on.

So how exactly did you set it up in practice?

There was a print out of all who had attended YFR, and we were able to get a copy. The church at Stoke and its overseers were very supportive. They funded the initial postage and stationery which we used to invite everyone from YFR to participate - at least those for whom we had an address. It was also necessary to include instructions about how this new prayer scheme would work. Individuals also sent gifts to help with the set-up and running costs. In some parts, it worked well, in others it inevitably fell apart. Transatlantic mailings were in no small way responsible for this. There certainly were frustrating delays in those early days of Prayer Mail's operation, but technology has changed a lot since then! The development of computers and email soon started to make a difference.

As more and more people began to get e-mail addresses, the scheme then became known as Prayer Email. The biggest change being that, rather than needing to circulate mailings, there could now be one central point from which all the prayer requests could be sent out digitally by computer.

Why do people often refer to Prayer Mail as 'Deckspear'?

It's a combination of a shortened form of Derek - 'Deck' - and 'Spear' from the full business name, 'Spear Travels'. 'Deckspear' was the email address from which the prayer points were sent out and it just 'stuck', no doubt being reinforced because, at that time, 1993/94, I was the first person known to many of my friends as having an email address! Just exactly when it became known as Prayer Email is difficult to determine.

Can you tell us something about the scale of the operation?

There are currently 440 addresses around the globe receiving the emails direct. I know of some instances where the emails are then forwarded to or printed out for others. It's common enough for them to be used in church prayer meetings. However, I don't really have any definite idea of the number of people they actually reach. I would estimate that a fair percentage of people belonging to the Churches of God in the western world have made some use of Prayer Mail since it began way back in 1992.

Has there been any particular time when you realized just how effective Prayer Email was?

I remember the time when I realized how instantaneous it could be. It was when Mary and John Kerr were struck by a car. Since I am able to keep an eye on emails while working, I was able to immediately pick up an email which came through from the family saying that Mary was going into surgery and so prayer was being urgently requested. It struck me that in less than a minute I had received and forwarded on that request, and that forwarded request in turn could then have been opened and read as far away as Australia, enabling people to pray for Mary while she was still in surgery.

Can you give us some idea of the volume of work involved in running the scheme?

How much Prayer Email is used is determined by everyone who is involved, not by me. The percentage of contributors is minimal compared to the number who actually receive the emails. The scope of its use is also down to others. From my point of view, there are some very quiet weeks when next to nothing is received; but, equally, other weeks can be very busy with several prayer requests being received daily.

FISCAL FIASCOS AND THE SATANIC SOLUTION (MARTIN JONES)

Shocked European bankers are taking huge losses on their investments in the Greek economy; whilst European governments reluctantly put their hands deep into their pockets just to keep the Euro dream afloat. But, if either had paid more attention in history class, this whole fiasco might have been avoided, or at least the early warnings recognized. In the context of taking an investment gamble, the Greek horse had form.

Since independence from the Ottoman Empire in 1832, Greece has suffered recurring budget crises, frequent state defaults and long periods during which it has effectively been cut off from the international capital markets. Despite that, its current membership of the Euro isn't the first time that an ill-advised attempt has been made to unify it with its neighbours. Latin Monetary Union (LMU) was attempted in 1866 between France, Belgium, Italy and Switzerland; not by a new coinage, but by pegging each currency at the same fixed rate. Greece joined two years later. Britain, true to form, would have nothing to do with it and was proved absolutely correct. The Greek government propped up their ailing economy by gradually decreasing the amount of gold in their coins - that rendered the fixed rate meaningless. Things got so bad that Greece was formally expelled from the LMU in 1908 and the whole scheme was soon to be wrecked by the upheaval of World War One.

The irony of the historical and current situation isn't lost on students of ancient history, who point out that the Greeks were pioneers of economic and monetary union. In 400 B.C., seven Greek states minted coins to the same weight with a common design (of the baby Heracles strangling a snake) and the first three letters of the Greek word for 'alliance'. Like today, each state placed its own particular image on the reverse. Why it collapsed after 200 years is unknown, but the Achaean League had another go in about 280 B.C. using the head of Zeus as the common design.

The historian Polybius noted that there was more than monetary union. They "had not only formed an allied and friendly community, but they have the same laws, weights, measures and coinage, as well as the same officials, council and courts of justice"; enough, perhaps, to make today's Eurocrats green with envy - but it lasted barely a century due to the crushing defeat by the Romans at the Battle of Corinth in 146 B.C.

History is littered with aborted attempts at economic and monetary union; a track record that led Walter Bagehot, the essayist and editor of The Economist, to write in the late 1860s - "the attempt to found a universal money is not possible now." He concluded that the practical difficulties were "simply insurmountable." Based simply on current events, that assessment seems to be well supported -what chance of a global system when even a regional one is fragile? It is not hard to find one of the main causes of these repeated failures. Paul put his finger on it with his warning to the Church of God in Philippi: *Do nothing out of selfish ambition or vain conceit, but in humility consider others better than yourselves. Each of you should look not only to your own interests, but also to the interests of others.* [1]

In 'normal circumstances', union can only be achieved when we act responsibly, unselfishly and for the greater good - and, by the way, that's just as true in our churches as it is at inter-governmental level. That little caveat is necessary, for students of the Bible will be well aware that Bagehot's view will one day be proved to be incorrect - but it will be unity achieved for the greater evil, not the good. Rev.13:16 speaks of a universal regulated trading system, not denoted by the head of Zeus or Heracles, but by the name or number of 'the beast'. No currency will be usable without it. The carrots of economic and social stability and the sticks of persecution and execution will make it tough to keep out of this diabolical pact - but taking the mark of the Antichrist will have eternal consequences by permanently aligning the taker against the true Christ and in union with Satan.

The Bible teaches that Christians will be spared from these events, later enjoying instead the wonderful millennial unity pictured by the wolf living with the lamb.[2] But we should be alert to the reality that men and women around us are hurtling towards something far worse than mere economic meltdown. We must trigger the most reliable and timely 'early-warning' system - the plan of salvation in God's Word.

References: (1) Phil.2:3-4 NIV (2) Isa.11:6

S IS FOR... SEPARATION - WHAT, WHY, HOW? (GEOFF HYDON)

It all began with separation. Your Christian life started with action by God to set you apart. The Bible uses the word sanctification, and calls those who are sanctified: 'saints'. Essentially saints are those who have been set apart by God in holiness at the time they became children of God,[1] spiritually separated out from everyone else. Although God achieves that initial separation for us, He also expects those whom He makes saints to then live saintly lives and enjoy nearness to Him. That requires a constant readiness to set oneself apart for God to use, as enabled by the Holy Spirit. In the purpose of God, individual saints should practise their faith with fellow saints who are equally committed to serving the Lord from a pure heart.[2]

Churches of God are a practical necessity for this to happen, and to continue to reflect this corporate reality such churches must themselves retain their distinctiveness by keeping themselves separate from error (motivated strongly by the awareness that God is dwelling among them).[3] Could you affirm and explain these matters from Scripture? This article is intended to help with that by briefly covering the What, Why and How of separation and provide lots of scriptural references to enable you to check out the context and do more general reading on this subject.[4]

What?

It's a two-sided coin and its essence could hardly be better expressed than Paul's instruction to Timothy: now *(1) flee from youthful lusts* and *(2) pursue righteousness, faith, love and peace, with those who call on the Lord from a pure heart.*[5] Note, separation from others' sins[6] and errors is not merely theoretical, it will require action in relation to the people committing them (and thus the cautions of Gal.6:1 and 2 Tim.2:24-25 are necessary.)

For landmark guidance on this subject we first go to 2 Corinthians, which deals primarily with separation from unbelievers, and clarifies the stark spiritual differences between saved and unsaved, no matter how great their sins or how good their good deeds.[7] This is not to minimize the responsibility we have towards all people, no matter what their transgressions; just to remember the focus the Lord expects.[8] And is it true of you and me that we have first ensured that we ourselves are pure,[9] through cessation of sins, repentance and cleansing through confession?[10]

But the Lord's spotless life confirms that separation is not just about where you are or who you are with.[11] In 1 Cor.5:11 the instruction to not 'associate' with certain sinning people means more than just being with them, it literally means to not be mixed up[12] with them; if we are indistinguishable from them our witness for Christ is compromised.[13] So separation means avoiding being harmfully mixed with others, for a greater goal. This evidently should govern the 'why' and 'how' as well as the 'what' and 'where' of our actions.

Now when writing to the Thessalonian church, Paul instructed the believers to choose not to mix with certain people in the church, for the purpose of error-correction.[14] That is very challenging as each of us considers our own weaknesses, and the practical issues around putting this beneficial and non-optional instruction into effect. And the principle obviously must apply to relationships with believers not in a church of God too; wrong does not become right based on that distinction. Beloved fellow believers, and churches they may attend, can be caught up in various kinds of error, which don't mix with true obedience to the Word of God.

What should we particularly watch out for? The errors will usually fall into one of three main categories: wrong teaching; wrong activity; or the right activity but done by the wrong people. Most commonly seen errors in these categories would include:

(1) Doctrinal error: compromise of the whole counsel of God;[15] assuming that either water baptism is required for salvation, or that it is not necessary for disciples at all; thinking salvation can be lost (falling away),[16] teaching salvation by works;[17] making no distinction between 'the church, which is His (Christ's) Body'[18] and a Church of God.[19]

(2) Sinful practices: worldliness,[20] idleness/misuse of time/effort,[21] idolatry,[22] immorality;[23]

(3) People problems: Autocratic or independent church leadership;[24] women in authority or teaching positions in the church.[25]

Obviously, more could be added, but these are encountered frequently and signal the need for separation, for such things should not be present in a church of God. This is not to say that churches of God are free from error, for they are composed of believers who are as prone as any others to sin and getting things wrong. However, the New Testament pattern for the operation of a church of God is intended to ensure that it is kept free from such things.[26]

Why?

To be in fellowship with God requires us to walk in the light.[27] Practically, the disciple who is seeking closeness to God will also be drawn to fellowship with those of like mind. Are these your personal goals? To respond to a natural question about why churches of God need to be separate from other churches, even strongly evangelical ones, we can find an answer in actual experience. In the late 1800s many saints separated from Brethren companies in order to form new churches of God. Why? This was not based on dislike of the people, or failure to recognize that there was much to be admired in them. The disciples that withdrew did so because they saw that there were fundamental practices to be followed in order to conform to the scriptural description of a church of God, and there was behaviour that was appropriate in the house of God.[28] These things simply could not be achieved in the Brethren churches as they were.

Scripture requirements about church functions, even those as basic as Acts 2:42, need to be adopted unitedly by saints; an individual cannot implement them alone. Nor could the Brethren churches be corrected, because the scripturally-based form of leadership and the decision-making process required to resolve the problems were absent, indeed resisted.[29] The only solution then was for faithful disciples to purge themselves from their former association in the spirit of 2 Tim.2:19-22, even though that course was very painful for them. We must of course take care now not to become transgressors by reversing such a stance.[30]

That could occur if, by participating with churches that are in error, we effectively align ourselves with their wrong teaching or condone their erroneous practices, and so build up the wrong thing. The correct answer is to continually attempt to testify to the truth, with a prayerful desire that our contacts will want to uphold that truth with us. In turn that requires the churches of God to be fully submissive to the Holy Spirit's guidance into all the truth from the Scriptures.[31]

How?

There is no option but to continually base our action on what we find in the Word of God.[32] Separation may seem unwelcome if we fail to implement it with a view to getting closer to God, or if we give priority to our popularity! (Remember, the effect of Christ's sinless life on others was to condemn sin in the flesh, and He is our example.[33]) Correspondingly, it is the Holy Spirit's application of the truth that brings about our daily sanctification.[34] The Scriptures will alert us not only to error but to what is excellent and worthy of the full occupation of our thoughts, in all we do.[35] This mind-set is needed so that we act in mercy and grace, in truth and love,[36] neither compromising our walk[37] nor blindly cutting ourselves off from the needs of our fellow men. Most comforting is the fact that the place of separation is not a lonely one; God calls us to it, so by definition He is already there.[38] The attitude of Moses in this matter must be ours;[39] the presence of the Lord is the goal of separation.

Is being separate too limiting? When you are part of a thriving church with lots going on, it is easier to find your social needs satisfied in friendships and activities with fellow Christians there. What if you are seeking a life partner, but with no obvious prospects in your local church? Or what if you have a zeal for evangelism but you are in a church of God that is small, ageing and with little outreach activity? Still this truth of separation must apply. It constrains you no more in making worthwhile contacts and serving the Lord than it did the Apostles! It will help you to unselfishly hone your vision of a key life-goal: bringing others as close to the Lord as you yourself desire to be. Separation is neither an excuse for inactivity, nor a justification for griping about things; it is a central truth that provides a proper basis for fellowship the Lord desires to bless!

References: (1) 2 Thess.2:13 (2) 2 Tim.2:22 (3) 2 Cor.13:5; 1
Cor.3:16-17 (4) For more reading on this subject, please obtain copies
of *The Search for the Truth of God* and *Churches of God, New Testament
Pattern,* available from www.HayesPress.org[1] (5) 2 Tim.2:22, bracketed
numbers added (6) 1 Tim.5:22; Eph.5:11 (7) 2 Cor.6:14-7:1. See also
2 Tim.3:1-5; 1 Jn 2:15; Jas.4:4 (8) Jn 17:11-19 (9) Matt.7:3-5 (10) 1
Jn 1:9 (11) Matt.9:10-13 (12) Gk. *sunanamignumi* 'to mix up with'
(An Expository Dictionary of New Testament Words, W.E. Vine) (13)
Matt.5:13 (14) 2 Thess.3:6-15 (15) Acts 20:20-21,27 (16) Jn 10:28
(17) Eph.2:8-9 (18) Eph.1:23 (19) 1 Cor.1:2 See NT Issue 4, 2011, p.6
and NT Issue 1,2012, p.15 (20) Tit.2:12; Jude 1:19 (21) 2 Thess.3:11
(22) 1 Cor.5:11 (23) 1 Cor.6:18 (24) 3 Jn 9-11; Tit.l:5ff (25) 1
Tim.2:12 (26) 1 Cor.5:6-7; 2 Cor.7:1 (see also Footnote 4) (27) 1 Jn
1:6-8 (28) 1 Tim.3:15 and see footnote 2 above (29) See *Elders and The
Elderhood,* especially chapter 8, available from www.HayesPress.org[2]
(30) Gal.2:18 (31) Jn 16:13; 17:17 (32) Acts 17:11 (33) Rom.8:3-8
(34) Jn 17:17 (35) Phil.4:8 (36) Col.4:5-6 (37) Phil.3:16; 4:9; 2
Tim.3:14 (38) 2 Cor.6:17 implied in the translation 'Come' (39)
Ex.33:12-16

Bible quotes from NASB

---

1. http://www.HayesPress.org

2. http://www.HayesPress.org

MISSION: WARMED-UP HEART OF AFRICA (BENNET NTAMBALIKA)

Whoever would have thought that a simple enquiry by Patson Katimba in 1983 about a Churches of God publication would eventually lead to the planting of such Churches in Malawi? *"As for God His way is perfect."* [1] Correspondence between Patson and Alan Toms continued for a long time and then was passed on to the Fellowship Outreach Committee. Patson shared copies of the magazine with friends and they were used as study guides at their fellowship meetings. Unsurprisingly, because the group enjoyed the teaching so much, they requested people be sent to Malawi to teach the truth the magazine was propagating.

Mark Imoukhuede and Godwin Okwena from Nigeria met Patson sometime in 1995 at the Airport holding a copy of the Needed Truth (NT) magazine. Today there are many names on the mailing list from all over the country. During an International Trade Fair when the Churches of God had a stand, the Needed Truth magazine was an attraction, not just because of its new look, but because of its heart-warming content. Testimonies abound of the impact NT magazine has had on many lives. We pray that from Malawi, the Warm Heart of Africa, the hearts of men and women will be warmed up as they read this magazine.

From that time Nigerian brethren and also evangelist 'Uncle' Bernard French made frequent follow-up visits to the work of God which had started in Malawi. The truths concerning the teachings of the Churches of God were taught to those people who were showing interest until 1999 when the first Church of God was planted in Chilomoni, Blantyre City. Through crusade meetings conducted around Blantyre City, many people gladly received the Word of God and were baptised.

This led to the planting of another Church of God in Ndirande, Blantyre. God continued to be gracious to the people of Malawi and the work began to spread to the remote areas such as Ntcheu, Mulanje and Milepa in Chiradzulu District where Churches of God were also planted.

The work of God is still growing and spreading to other areas where people are showing interest such as Lilongwe, the Capital city of Malawi; Lumbazi, a township in Lilongwe; Bangwe, in the city of Blantyre; Nyezerela and Chinama in Phalombe District; and Mulumba in Mulanje District. God has continued to provide spiritually for His people in Malawi, but has also made provision for the people physically. In 2008 the so-called 'UK 3', Norma Aitken, Karl Smith and his wife, Joy, came to Malawi in order to find ways and means how those in the churches could become self-reliant and disease-free. These three people did a tremendous job. They worked tirelessly, travelling to the remotest areas even though the weather was not suited to westerners. They met with different government officials to find out ways in which the people of Malawi could be assisted with physical needs such as good water, enough food, healthy lives and education in order to make their lives better.

We thank God for the following developments which the UK 3 achieved during their stay in Malawi and for the ways in which those in the churches have benefited:

(1) The saints, including the surrounding community, were provided with seeds and fertilizers and trained in modern farming techniques. The following year the saints had enough food to eat and the surplus was sold.

(2) Adult literacy schools were opened in all the five churches to help those who could not write and to help them read their Bibles.

(3) Mobile clinics were opened to help those who live in remote assemblies without access to government clinics, dispensaries and medical facilities.

(4) An orphanage school was opened at Ndirande, providing breakfast, lunch and medical care.

Reference: (1) 2 Sam.22:31 NIV

TWITCHING! (GILBERT GRIERSON)

My brother, a bird-watcher (or 'twitcher'), was excited. We had brought him out on a two-day trip to Donegal on the west coast of Ireland. Having found a hostel to stay in, we set off to explore the area with its wild rocky fells, high cliffs, deserted beaches and Atlantic breakers. With nothing between us and America except water, we set off to walk along the beach.

While his binoculars were trained on two large black birds feeding on the cliff-side grass which he identified as being a rare species and which caused him great excitement (he was twitching all over!), my attention was drawn to a flock of sheep which were also grazing on the grassy slopes that tumbled down to the beach. They were on the move. I spotted the shepherd before I saw his dogs. There were two of them, black and white collies, working hard, perfectly coordinated, running this way, pausing, lying down, running back the other way, skilfully coercing the sheep in the required direction and collecting up any strays. The shepherd's shouts and whistles gave the dogs their orders, and these, obviously well-trained, responded to their master's voice. This was a beauty to behold in their perfect obedience.

Their master's voice! There was a time when THE Master's voice was heard in this world, sometimes loud and authoritative, saying, *"Peace, be still!"*[1] quietening the raging sea; sometimes gently and lovingly saying, *"Come to Me"*.[2] What a privilege to listen to Jesus' voice and converse with Him face to face! The incarnate Word was revealing the heart and mind of the invisible God. There were times for questions - there's nothing wrong with questions as they can reveal a healthy, inquisitive mind. But there were other times when, the Bible says, *from that day on no one dared to ask him any more questions.* [3] Yes, there is: *A time to keep silence, And a time to speak.* [4]

Healthy asking must turn to quietly trusting. There are some things that our Master speaks to us about that we will never understand fully down here -things which *we see in a mirror, dimly.* [5] Then it is a time for resting on faith. After all, we don't see the whole picture down here and some knowledge is too deep for us; such as how and where the Good Shepherd is leading His sheep, going on ahead, calling, not driving with dogs. At times all we hear Him say is, *"Follow Me."* [6] He will not take us where He will not go Himself. *"I am with you always."* [7] So we ...'Trust and obey, for there's no other way, To be happy in Jesus, but to trust and obey.'[8]

I felt led that day on the beach in Donegal to bend down and write something in the sand with a stick before we left the sea-shore and climbed the 167 steps to the cliff top and went on our way. What did I write? **JESUS IS LORD.** And He is. Lord of the sand, sea, cliffs, rare birds, sheep, men and women, boys and girls; Lord of all. The Atlantic breakers came in later that day and washed away that truth written in the sand, but one day the Master's voice will be heard again on earth and at His name every knee will bow, and every tongue will confess that Jesus Christ is Lord, to the glory of God the Father.[9] That truth will never be erased for the whole of eternity. Now that really is something to start 'twitching' about!

References: (1) Mk.4:39 (2) Matt.11:28 (3) Matt.22:46 NIV (4) Eccles.3:7 (5) 1 Cor.13:12

(6) e.g. Matt.4:19 (7) Matt.28:20 (8) John H. Sammis (9) Phil.2:10-11

Bible quotations from NKJV unless otherwise stated

IS IT MARRIAGE OR NOT? (PETER HICKLING)

How do you find out what a word means? Look in a dictionary, of course! But the trouble with this is that a dictionary will say what a word means to most people now, not what it has meant, or what its derivation implies. For example, take the word 'gay'; the Shorter Oxford English Dictionary of 1964 gives its primary meaning as 'Full of or disposed to joy or mirth; light-hearted...', a meaning current since the 14th century. Yet the current O.E.D. on iPod gives the primary meaning as '(of a person, especially a man) homosexual', and describes the long-standing meaning as 'dated'. The word has been hijacked and given a substituted meaning such that it is not now possible to use it in its traditional sense without provoking sniggers.

The meaning of the word 'marriage' is now under threat, when some want to redefine it to accommodate their ideas about acceptable behaviour. The iPod O.E.D. does give the accepted understanding of this: 'The formal union of a man and woman, typically as recognised by law, in which they become husband and wife'. This, too, has been the normal usage of the last 800 years. Now some would like to apply the term 'marriage' to arrangements between people of the same sex. The simplest objection to this is that it is not what the word means. For example, you may have a red car, and you know what this means; someone else can't come up with a blue car and say 'Mine is red too, because I say so'.

It is legal in some jurisdictions for people of the same sex to register civil partnerships, which give them the same fiscal and legal status as married people, but they cannot truly be called married, because that is not what the word means. Why should we bother about this? Because it is another attempt to take a generally understood word, and wrest it from its normal meaning. The homosexual lobby keeps trying to do this, hoping that deviant behaviour will come to be seen as simply a lifestyle choice, which can be described using the same terms that we have always used for normal behaviour. This is not true; a man and woman together can naturally procreate children, which a homosexual pair cannot.

But this is a Christian magazine, and there are far more important reasons for the endorsement of marriage than traditional or practical ones. We stand by the Biblical teaching about marriage, expressed right through the Old and New Testaments. At the very beginning God said, *Therefore, a man shall leave his father and his mother and hold fast to his wife, and they shall become one flesh*[1], and the Lord Jesus Himself quoted this. It is true that some of the patriarchs and Israelites had multiple wives. This was permitted, although not encouraged. New Testament times show a return to the divine ideal. Jesus attended and made wine for the wedding feast at Cana of Galilee[2], and everywhere the New Testament assumes the one-man-one-woman relationship as the norm. Scripture goes further, and parallels the relationship between husband and wife with that between Christ and the Church[3].

Someone may say, 'Yes, that's all right for you. You are a Christian, and accept the Bible's rules; but I am not. You go your way, and I'll go mine'. We say 'Do what you will, though we don't think you should, but whatever arrangement you make, you can't call it marriage, because that isn't what the word means.' Whether secular opponents like it or not the English language has been built up on the foundation of Christian beliefs, and if people want to adopt different practices they must find different words for them. We are thinking of an English word, of course, but the same would apply to the corresponding word in other languages. What we are really standing up for is the recognition of marriage as an institution, in its customary and biblical sense.

References: (1) Gen.2:24 ESV (2) Jn 2:1-11 (3) Eph.5:22-33

TAKING A STAND - AN INTERVIEW WITH JACK MCILVENNA, MIDDLESBROUGH, ENGLAND

Why did you take a stand as a Conscientious Objector?

Although the Second World War had ceased about seven years earlier, the U.K. still had conscription legislation in force. This meant that unless you were in employment that was considered to be of national importance, or still in full-time education, you were required to engage in military service. However, there was also in force legislation that permitted you to register as a Conscientious Objector. As a teenager I was well aware of the issues involved in this and was absolutely convinced that as a follower of the Lord Jesus Christ it would be wrong for me to serve in a military capacity.

Which scriptures guided your thoughts?

The main scriptures I used during the proceedings were *pursue peace with all people;[1] be diligent to be found by Him in peace;[2]* and *love your enemies ... and pray for those who ... persecute you.* [3]

Were you apprehensive: did you doubt at any point that this was the right course of action?

Yes, I was apprehensive, but I believed strongly that I would be failing the Lord if did anything other than take a stand on this matter. In this connection I was strongly influenced by the Lord's words, *"he who does not take his cross and follow after Me is not worthy of Me."[4]*

What actually happened at the tribunal: what was the process?

In order for the process to begin you had to register at your local Employment Exchange as a conscientious objector. Two months after I registered I appeared before my first tribunal hearing in Glasgow. I think this consisted of a panel of five, one of whom chaired the proceedings. I was required to state my reasons for requesting registration as a Conscientious Objector, following which a Christian brother witnessed to my beliefs. Then followed detailed questioning designed to examine my resolution and make me justify my reasons. The panel then conferred for a few minutes after which they stated that I would be required to engage in military service in a non-combatant capacity. I appealed against this decision and, six weeks later, I appeared before the Appeal Tribunal in Edinburgh. The same process was followed, but on this occasion the decision was that my name be removed from the Register of Conscientious Objectors resulting in me being required to undertake Military Service of a combatant nature.

What arguments and pressures were brought to bear during the proceedings?

The members of the tribunal argued that the Bible was a book full of war; Jesus Himself said, *"I did not come to bring peace but a sword"*[5] and, *"he who has no sword, let him sell his garment and buy one."* [6] the Bible teaches that, *the authorities that exist are appointed by God*[7] and *submit yourselves to every ordinance of man for the Lord's sake.*[8]" Would you, a strong young man, stand and watch your mother being killed and do nothing about it?"

What was the procedure following this?

I was required to attend for a medical to assess my suitability for Military Service, the health questioner including a section in which I was required to enter the regiment I would like to join. I wrote, "As a follower of the Lord Jesus Christ I cannot take part in Military

Service." This was strongly disputed by the Army Medical Officer who was responsible for coordinating the medical results, however I was adamant that I was not prepared to change my statement. Following this I received my 'call-up' papers to report for Military Service. I then wrote to the Commanding Officer to inform him of my strongly held beliefs. He replied that it would be dealt with when I reported to the Army barracks.

How did others treat you?

There was a strong anti-war feeling amongst the general population at this time, so neighbours and colleagues had a grudging admiration for my 'stand'. However this was certainly not the case at the Army barracks, where shouting, threats and persuasion were used to try to force me to sign documents and to wear an army uniform. In an effort to discharge me without involving military discipline, I was hospitalised in the sick bay in order for me to be examined by a psychiatrist. A week later the psychiatric examination findings were that there was no reason for me being declared unfit for Military Service. Although I had argued strongly against being hospitalised, the Lord had a purpose in it, for I was granted permission with the complete agreement of the patients to preach at a Gospel service which all the soldiers attended.

What was the most difficult moment?

I was subsequently charged and placed under close arrest. This lasted for a week and was the worst part of the whole experience for I was kept in a small cell, deprived of all my mail and visited by an Army Chaplain every day. He spent hours with me trying to persuade me to become a soldier and threatening me that otherwise I would remain in that cell indefinitely. By the end of the week I was in despair, but thankfully I had been permitted to keep my Bible, and as I read it the following words 'jumped off the page': *At my first defense no one stood with me, but all forsook me ... But the Lord stood with me and strengthened me ... Also I was delivered out of the mouth of the lion.*[9]

Despair became joy, as I fell on my knees before the Lord and thanked Him for speaking to me so clearly. The next day everything changed, I was placed under open arrest and, with certain restrictions, was allowed to engage in normal daily activities within the Army camp, to write and receive correspondence and to even have visitors.

How did you sense the Lord's hand with you, helping you?

The Lord provided an Army captain who understood the reasons for my stand, so I requested that he become my Defending Officer. He ensured that I would be given a sentence of 96 days, as this was the legal requirement in order to be able to appeal to another tribunal. He also requested that I serve my sentence in the Detention Centre of the Army barracks to avoid having a criminal record. He later agreed to attend the final tribunal in London to support my plea. The outcome of this tribunal was that they recommended to the War Office that I be discharged from the Army and serve 2 years and 3 months on 'work of National importance'.

On my return home I obtained employment on a local estate as a forester, later leaving there to become a nursing assistant in a hospital for elderly people. In the Bible that went with me throughout that year I underlined *rejoicing that they were counted worthy to suffer shame for His name*[10] as I, too, felt that I had been privileged in that way.

References: (1) Heb.12:14 (2) 2 Pet.3:14 (3) Matt.5:44 (4) Matt.10:38 (5) Matt.10:34 (6) Lk.22:36 (7) Rom.13:1 (8)1 Pet.2:13 (9) 2 Tim.4:16-17 (10) Acts 5:41

Bible quotations from NKJV

MISSION: LIGHT IN THE DARKNESS (GERALDE MAG-USARA)

In a recent mission trip, about eight hundred people in total heard the gospel and God's plan for our discipleship (in the 7 steps of Acts 2:41,42) throughout six barangays (villages): Pantukan, Kaligutan, Sonlon, Liguyon, Nabunturan and Salvador. Local brothers in each place have committed to following them up. Due to stormy weather, we were detained for two days preaching from house to house and conducting Bible studies where we were. In this, God overruled because a 25 year-old, five months pregnant, was suddenly gripped by the truth of God's Word. She texted her boyfriend and declared they must cease living together for Christ's sake (Lk.9:23). It will be far from easy, but we pray that she may overcome her difficult situation with God's help. "I would like to be in God's house," she said.

Fifteen persons recently observed the breaking of the bread - may the Lord add them to God's house! They came from the area surrounding our hall in Davao, some walking for almost an hour to observe how to remember the Lord in the biblical Breaking of the Bread as practised in the Churches of God. God has used our preaching with the (data) projector as a tool to show the light of salvation to about 40 people in one physically and spiritually dark area. Now we are very busy in follow-up work there among the 300 people of that village.

At another nearby location, we also preached with it. The people there, like me, are poor on earth, but rich in heaven because more than ten people there repented and accepted Christ as personal Saviour. Most of the people there live without electric light. I feel they are more receptive than the richer ones in the immediate vicinity of our hall.

In two further nights of evangelizing using the laptop and data projector, at another spot close to the Davao church hall, seventeen people received Christ as their personal Saviour. I hope the Lord will add them to His house. I wish God would send more workers to help in the follow-up.

WHY A WOMAN SHOULD COVER HER HEAD IN CHURCH (BRIAN JOHNSTON)

[3] But I want you to understand that Christ is the head of every man, and the man is the head of a woman, and God is the head of Christ.... [5]But every woman who has her head uncovered while praying or prophesying disgraces her head, for she is one and the same as the woman whose head is shaved. ... [6] let her cover her head. "For a man ought not to have his head covered, since he is the image and glory of God; but the woman is the glory of man.... [10] the woman ought to have a symbol of authority on her head. (1 Cor.11:3-10 NASB)

The issue

The purpose of this article is to defend the teaching and practice of head-covering by women in the churches of God. It is claimed[1] that in the Roman Empire, around the time of the New Testament, a dress code developed: it became a case of 'you are what you wear.' At a time when women were gaining financial power and control over their lives, some chose to go about bare-headed, flaunting elaborate hairdos[2] and challenging convention. High-class married women, tempted to conform to this image of the 'new woman', might then have been among those leading the challenge against the wearing of head coverings at Corinth.

As for any factors which may have influenced male behaviour, sculptures exist which show those taking an active part in pagan rituals did so with their head covered. Generally, male pagan priests at Corinth were drawn from the social elite. This raises the possibility that active brothers in the Corinthian church were likewise divisively stressing their nobility[3] by covering their heads. While these points are of interest in getting a feel for what may have raised the question at Corinth, we will see that the all-encompassing nature of the apostle Paul's answer shows local and cultural matters - then and now - to be beside the point.

A major interpretive key:

A man ought not to have his head covered because he is *the image and glory of God.*[4] This description of man is something seen in the creation account[5] and is traceable throughout the Bible.[6] It is a major interpretive key for 1 Cor.11:2-16, the significance of which is all too readily overlooked. For if a man ought not to have his head covered because he is the image and glory of God, then clearly these instructions go way beyond any local or cultural boundary, and must have relevance for all brothers and sisters in the churches of God[7] at any time and place where they exist.

It is worth emphasizing that the key point of man being the image and glory of God is applied to the actual symbol of head-covering. The insertion of verses 8 and 9 into the flow of the argument in 1 Cor.11 serves at first sight to make the parallel (see inset box below) of verse 7 with verse 10 less obvious. The wording of that latter verse is admittedly difficult, but in any event, it has to mean that a woman should wear a head covering, for nothing else is a satisfactory punch-line to the argument which Paul has been advancing. In each case, God alone gets the glory!

We may conclude that these instructions about head-coverings mean:

(1) a man wears no covering for he is God's glory: this means God's glory is uncovered, even as God is subject to no-one.

(2) a woman wears a covering for she is man's glory: this means man's glory is covered, even as man is subject to Christ - and so the glory again goes to God instead. And,

(3) a woman wears a covering: which also means that her personal glory (her hair) is covered. So, women cover their heads (and men uncover theirs) in order that God gets the glory in each case in accordance with the hierarchical authority structure of verse 3. It has been suggested that the word 'head' in this passage carries the meaning of source. The case for this is weak, but even if it were so, surely the thought would have to be that of an authority source or structure related to the content of the verses which follow.

A major rule in biblical interpretation

To handle God's Word accurately we first need to study what the text meant to the original hearers. So, what did Paul mean when he wrote, *Every man who has something on his head while praying or prophesying disgraces his head. But every woman who has her head uncovered while praying or prophesying disgraces her head?*[8] How was this understood in earliest Christian times?

The English Standard Version Bible (ESV) seems to imply that, in New Testament times, women's head covering in 1 Cor.11 may have symbolized marital status. Is there any substance to this suggestion? In fact, the early Christian practice of head-covering by single as well as married women is reflected in non-biblical writings.[9] It is also supported by second and third century pictures from the catacombs showing Christian women praying with a cloth veil on their heads. Paul's Greek word means 'thoroughly covered'. Some propose that it is a particular ('piled up in a bun') hairstyle that is in question,[10] however, the word used generally refers to a covering of some kind.[11] The corresponding male prohibition in 1 Cor.11:4, against having (literally) 'something down from the head,' occurs in this exact form in the Greek version of the Old Testament in Est.6:12 when Haman covered his head in shame, surely using part of his clothing to do so.

What does our human nature teach us (1 Cor.11:14)?

As in Rom.1:26, this teaching warns against any blurring of the distinct roles appointed by God for male and female genders. God created humanity as *male and female,* and any move (such as women adopting what are perceived as male characteristics in their hairstyle) which lessens the impact of this God-given differentiation is not from God. Having established the authority structure as it applies between the sexes - which God wishes to be kept visibly distinct - the teaching of 1 Cor.11 on head coverings should be viewed as symbolizing this authority structure.

Where does this teaching on head coverings apply?

The teaching of 1 Cor.11:4-13 applies to those occasions when the church comes *together as a church* (lit. 'in church') since:

(a) Paul speaks of prophesying throughout this section of Corinthians (see 1 Cor.11:4,5) as delivering edification for the whole church;[12]

(b) In verse 11 the expression 'in the Lord' indicates the functioning of churches of God as in 1 Thess.5:12 - the context of instruction which is 'in

the Lord' in these instances (also 1 Cor.14:26) seems to most naturally relate to the instruction of a church of God when it is gathered in-church;

(c) 1 Cor.11:16 describes it as a church practice (a 'practice' is unmistakably a 'church' practice when it is viewed in the context of church gatherings);

(d) 'this instruction' (1 Cor.11:17a) probably refers back to the preceding one about the head-dress of women, with transition to what follows and so its application would then be to be those times when the church comes together (1 Cor.11:17b) as a church (v.18). This view has its notable advocates,[13] perhaps because in 1 Cor.7:6, Paul uses the same Greek expression to clearly refer back to what precedes it;

(e) and finally, the succeeding verses (1 Cor.11:17-34) are devoted to the breaking of bread ordinance which is clearly designed for the whole church (v.22) when it is 'in church'.

The last word on head coverings

The force of 1 Cor.11:16 also is often underplayed. The final word in settling any residual contention was twofold: the apostles ('we') had *no other practice;* and notably neither did *the churches of God.* So, rather than this head covering practice being limited to Corinth at that time, as some allege; the reality was that this was everywhere practised throughout the churches of God in New Testament times - possibly everywhere except at Corinth!

References: (1) Bruce W. Winter, *Roman Wives, Roman Widows,* Eerdmans, 2003 (2) see 1 Tim.2:9 (3) 1 Cor.1:26 (4) 1 Cor.11:7 (5) Gen.1:26-27 (6) e.g. in Rom.3:23 & 2 Cor.3:18 (7) 1 Cor.11:16 (8) 1 Cor.11:4-5 (9) Tertullian, *The Ante-Nicene Fathers, Vol. 4: The Veiling of Virgins,* pp. 27-29,33 (10) Some, in proposing this, appeal to the fact that in the Greek version of the Old Testament the same word describes the leper's 'unloosed' hair in Lev.13:45; cp. Num.5:18 (11) e.g. Gen.38:15; Isa.6:2 (12) cp. 1 Cor.14:4,12,19,31 (13) F. F. Bruce (First and Second Corinthians, NCB, London, Oliphants, 1971, p. 108) sees 'touto' (this) in v. 17 as referring to what has preceded, as does J. Hering (The First Epistle of Saint Paul to the Corinthians, Eng. Tr. by A. W. Heathcote and P. J. Allcock, London, Epworth, 1962, p.111-12) and C. K. Barrett (A Commentary on the First Epistle to the Corinthians, HNTC, New York, Harper & Row, 1968, p.260). The view expressed in the article is also that found in Robertson's Word Pictures on 1 Cor.11:17.

PRAYING FOR OUR CHILDREN (DAVID WEBSTER)

We tend to pray most about the things that matter most to us. Our children matter to us in a big way, so we will almost certainly pray for them. From the moment a woman realises that she is carrying new life within her that child becomes very precious and so it is a true spiritual response to commit the child, its future and its care and upbringing to the Lord for His blessing. An unborn child is known by the Lord[1] and we can reverently commit the future into the hand of the God who sees.[2] Consider the following individual scenarios:

The little boy is sleeping soundly in his bed. Encouraged by the story of Hannah,[3] his mother watches and silently prays that the Lord will reveal Himself to the child and that he will become a disciple of the Lord Jesus. She sees the need for men who love their God and prays that her little boy might fill that role. The teenage girl is going through a rough time at school. She is finding it hard to fit in and make friends and her frustration is making her a difficult person to live with. Her parents pray for her, that the Lord will provide a good friend for her and that her Christian faith will become strong; that she will make good choices and be kept from the evil that is all around her. They pray for themselves, too, that they will have all the wisdom and patience to help her get through this.

Their son is going through a period of unemployment which has affected his confidence. Unable to assist directly, his parents pray that he will find work and that he will maintain his trust in the Lord, and continue to serve the Lord meanwhile. Their family, no longer children, have left home and the older son has children of his own. Their daughter no longer maintains a Christian lifestyle. Still the parents regularly pray for them. The concerns are different, of course, but they pray that this new family will be strong and that their grandchildren will learn to love the God who sustained them through all their lives. They pray for their daughter that she will return to her faith and that she will be given help meanwhile in pursuing her career.

We should never underestimate the significance of a Christian home and regularly bringing our families to the almighty God of heaven. The allusion to Timothy's Christian mother and grandmother[4] brings a Bible perspective to it. The Lord Jesus encouraged little children to come to Him when He was here[5] and is still interested when we bring our little ones (and big ones!) before *the throne of grace.*[6]

What, then, ought we to pray about? If a *wise son brings joy to his father, but a foolish son grief to his mother,*[7] then we should certainly pray for them to get wisdom. We want them to put their faith in the Lord Jesus, don't we? And become disciples, too; we will pray for those. We want them to be kept from being corrupted by the evil world they are living in. We will talk to God about that. We want them to be kept safe. God will hear our requests for safe-keeping. They need a good education. We'll ask God to provide one. In fact, bringing up a family is a real cause for anxiety, isn't it? God's Word tells us, *Do not be anxious about anything, but in everything, by prayer and petition, with thanksgiving, present your requests to God. And the peace of God, which transcends all understanding, will guard your hearts and your minds in Christ Jesus.*[8]

We want to 'guard' our children and our prayers for them 'guard' our hearts. Praying for our children, we take our natural anxieties and concerns and leave them with our heavenly Father.

Bible quotations are from the NIV

References: (1) See Gen.16:11-12 (2) Gen.16:13 (3)1 Sam.1:11 (4) 2 Tim.1:5 (5) Mk.10:14 (6) Heb.4:16 (7) Prov.10:1 (8) Phil.4:6-7

UNSOUGHT: (GILBERT GRIERSON)

A couple of years ago I happened to be passing along a road and over the wall was a field that had a stream running through it, with quite a steep bank down to the water from the level field. In the field were a neighbour's sheep with their lambs. One lamb had wandered away down the bank to the water's edge and seemed to be having difficulty getting back up. It was making a lot of noise. I didn't think too much about it as I walked on. Surely the lamb would eventually find a way up to rejoin its mother, or the farmer would spot the distressed lamb as he was checking his flock. A few days later I passed that way again and, being reminded of the lamb, I stopped and looked over the wall. The dead body of the lamb lay in the cold water. Rescue had never come.

In her autobiography,[1] Patricia St John, the author of so many books that have thrilled, challenged and taught children (and adults) over the years, and who writes from her own life experiences and missionary work in North Africa, includes a chapter about the Mission Hospital at Tangier in Morocco. She writes of the extreme difficulties of bringing the message of the gospel to the people of that Muslim land and of the work of the hospital in opening hearts through the provision of free medical help to the needy at a time when no other help was available.

She writes of the day that a poor Moorish child was brought into the hospital in the arms of her father from a distant tribal village. Nothing could be done for her, and she was taken out of the hospital by her father to an animals' hut (a *fundak*) to die in his arms - the only one she knows who loves her. This is her poem:-

FATIMA

'I will die in my father's arms' she said,

'Amid scenes and faces I know,

Where donkeys stamp in the Fundak yard

Where straw is scanty and the cobbles are hard,

And the vermined squatters cook on the shard,

'Tis there that I long to go.'

'Not among faces foreign and kind

Would I plunge to the straits of death,

But under heavens starry and free

In the well-known haunts of poverty,

Held to the heart that yearns for me

Would I yield up my rattling breath.'

And through broken speech shall the Questing Love

Surge to her last alarms,

That scorns no channel to heal and bless,

Unperceived, through man's gentleness;

She shall rest in her final helplessness

In the Everlasting Arms.

Loving, unloved; seeking, unsought;

Knowing, the while unknown;

Denied all access, pursuing His quest,

The tide steals in on her long unrest:

Through the peace of a father's ragged breast

He shall gather and bear His own.

So writes Patricia St John of this little lost lamb. Fatima finally dies in the arms of her poverty-stricken earthly father who loved her, but unseen, behind and underneath are the 'everlasting arms' of the Good Shepherd, for, *he will gather the lambs in his arms.*[2] It is strange how the Spirit of God can take a single word out of a poem, give it a different emphasis, and bring home a deep challenge to the heart of the reader. That's how it was for me. **'Unsought'** was the word. As a missionary, Patricia St John carried the message of the good news of a shepherd who laid down His life for the sheep to a people whose hearts were as stony as their land. Jesus loved, but few loved Him in return. He came, seeking those who were lost, but few were seeking Him. He was unsought, but He never stopped loving and seeking. And then the sadness came to my heart, along with the challenge: what of the lambs and sheep who are on the point of perishing today; men, women, boys and girls like the lamb in the neighbour's field that no-one cared enough about to save? Who will go to them and tell them of a loving Saviour? Is there no one willing to leave the 'ninety-nine' and go and look for the one who is lost? Another lover of souls, and especially the souls of little lost lambs, wrote:

'O for a passionate passion for souls,

O for a pity that yearns!

O for a love that loves unto death,

O for a fire that burns!' [3]

References:

(1) Patricia St John tells her own Story OM Publishing 1993. (2) Isa.40:11 ESV (3) Amy Carmichael, founder of the Dohnavur Fellowship in S. India which provided a home for little children, especially girls saved from a life of deified sin in the Hindu Temples

THE HIGGS BOSON - THE GOD PARTICLE? (PETER HICKLING)

There was great excitement among the usually staid ranks of particle physicists on July 4th 2012 when it was announced at CERN, the European Council for Nuclear Research, in Geneva that an elementary particle called the Higgs boson had been detected. It had been proposed as part of the Standard Model of particle physics, and it had been the target of a long search using the Large Hadron Collider. Why the excitement? Because it seemed to justify the Standard Model, and bring closer a unified scientific understanding of the universe. Yet it is not even certain that the particle detected is a Higgs boson, and the scientist making the announcement was suitably cautious.

What is the point of writing about this here? Hardly any readers will be particle physicists (neither is the writer), and the existence or otherwise of the particle will not make any difference even to technological workers. The reason is that in 1993 Nobel Physics prize-winner Leon Lederman published a popular science book on particle physics, *The God Particle: If the Universe is the Answer, What is the Question?* Lederman really implied no more than that the finding of this particle would help to establish a final understanding of the structure of matter, but the term is sensational and overstates the importance of the discovery. However, the words were seized upon by people who knew little of the subject and used it as though science had now found that there was no need for a God.

This is absurd. Science studies the things that are; its method is to record what happens, to formulate a theory which connects those events, then to test the theory against other observations. It may be substantiated for the time being, or found wrong or incomplete. No scientific theory can be regarded as unchallengeable. As an example,

Aristotle reasoned that for a body to be in motion it must have a force acting on it: Newton overturned this in 1687, publishing his three laws of motion, which now schoolchildren learn. These in turn have been superseded by special relativity, although this makes no difference in ordinary earthly things. The point that must be grasped is that science can only codify what happens; it cannot explain why it happens.

Even the most complete system of physics cannot give the reasons for things. For instance, my wife might say, "Why are all those papers on the dining room table?" and I might answer, rather obtusely, "Because the table is flat, and strong enough to carry the load." Although that answer is true, it isn't what she wanted to know: why I had left them there. Reasons, in this sense of the word, cannot come from the movement of elementary particles, which are essentially irrational, but they come from thoughts and actions. There can only be reason if there is an original Reason outside the individual human mind; this Reason is God.[1]

Thus, the name the 'God particle' for the Higgs boson does much more harm than good; it misleads those who bow down before the present-day god of science and gives them an excuse to avoid thought. Of course, if a complete theory of matter were arrived at it would not be at all destructive of faith in God and Christ. Lederman himself (a Jew) suggested that a fuller understanding would enable people to understand 'how beautiful is the universe God has made'.

References: (1) Col.l:16-17; Heb.11:3; Jn 1:1

THE ADVOCATE (STEPHEN MCCABE)

An advocate speaks on behalf of, or represents, another. Paul's letter to Philemon is such a beautiful picture of advocacy. Paul's pleading there is on behalf of the servant, Onesimus, to Philemon, his master. It is surely like our Lord and Master who pleads for us, His servants, when we, in our own strength, fall so easily into sin.

... my child ...[1]

Paul refers to Onesimus as his child. You may remember how Joseph brought Ephraim and Manasseh before Jacob.[2] It's a faint echo of the Lord bringing the fruit of His work before His Father. Jacob says, "*I never expected to see your face; and behold, God has let me see your offspring also* ".[3] Jesus, as advocate, presents us to His Father, the triumph of Calvary won, the horror of Calvary behind Him. Not only has the Father seen the face of the Son again, but He has seen those He has brought with Him - His offspring. When He speaks to the Father on our behalf, it is in the context of our being intimately associated with Him because we are His.

... my very heart ...[4]

Paul says that he is sending Onesimus, his very heart. The advocacy of Paul here, and more importantly, the advocacy of the Lord Jesus, is not a cold, detached thing. The word 'advocate' easily brings an image of courtroom drama to our minds with its legal association in our language. It is easy to picture a lawyer representing a client, where the lawyer leaves work to go home and leaves the case and its concerns in the office, forgets the client until he returns. But when the Lord Jesus speaks for us before the Father, remember that we are His very heart.

... was useless, but now useful ...[5]

Onesimus means 'useful', so Paul is starting his appeal to Philemon with a bit of a pun. But the point is serious - Onesimus could be useful to Philemon! Isn't it wonderful to think that we can be useful to the Father? Once we were useless, but now the Lord Jesus as advocate can recommend us before the Father. How useful are we actually being? It's very easy, as part of a church, to just drift along under the radar. If too many people in an assembly start doing that then the church loses direction. It would be awful to contemplate a church of God - a group of people called together to serve God in His house - becoming unprofitable to God. Let's not allow that to happen in our churches! We were once useless to God, but now we can be useful to Him through what Jesus has done - let's make sure we are.

... receive him as you would receive me ...[6]

What a beautiful thing for Paul to say. And he is asking a lot! Philemon knew Paul. He respected and loved him. Paul says, "For my sake, do the exact same for Onesimus." The Father loves the Son more completely than we can presently understand. The Lord Jesus speaks on our behalf to the Father - "Receive him, receive her, as you would receive me."

Elsewhere Paul says that we are *accepted in the Beloved.*[1] There is no more wonderful position to be in than that.

... whatever he owes, put that on my account - I will repay ...[8]

Onesimus is very likely to have stolen from Philemon, but Paul says that he will 'foot the bill'. The big difference in what the Lord Jesus does for us is that He has already paid. The old account was settled long ago.

So whenever the accuser, Satan, stands before God to point the finger,[9] there is one who speaks on my behalf- "That has been paid for, paid for by My own blood, My own life." Our advocate says, "Whatever he or she owes, that was put on My account. And it has been settled."

The great comfort of 1 Jn 2:1 is that if and when we do sin, and our potentially useful service for our Master is put at risk, we have one who speaks for us before God, so we have nothing to fear.

References: (1) Philn.1:10 (2) Gen.48:1,9 (3) Gen.48:11 (4) Philn.1:12 (5) Philn.1:11 (6) Philn.1:17 (7) Eph.1:6 NKJV (8) Phil.1:18-19 (9) Zech.3:1; Rev.12:10

Bible quotations from ESV unless otherwise stated

MILESTONES: AN INTERVIEW WITH SUZANNAH GOLDSACK, VICTORIA, CANADA

Each of our lives contains 'landmark' events in terms of God's dealings with us. It's biblically precedented that we should recall these, even as there were certain stones which were to 'become a memorial to the sons of Israel forever'.[1] Sue, tell us, what would you consider to be landmarks or 'memorial stones' in your life that you could share with us?

Memorial Stone 1: When my grandmother died, in the clear-out of her house, we found her mother's Bible, and in it, a photograph of me as a child, a baby on her lap. She had written: "This child is for the Lord."

Memorial Stone 2: When I was 15, my parents were having a difficult time in their marriage. My mother worked nights and my father worked days, just so they didn't have to see each other. My father suffered from post-traumatic stress syndrome. When seventeen, fighting in WW2 with the Navy, he was one of a few survivors on a ship that went down. He would neither see a psychiatrist, nor could he deal with the mental illness. So our family became the battleground. On February 18, 1970, my father called my brother, my sister and me into the room of our home and hugged us. The next day, my brother and I went to the garage. We opened the door, flipped on the lights, and found dad dead on the front seat of his car, having run a vacuum hose from the exhaust pipe into the car. Time stood still. Suicide is never about the victim, but about the survivors.

In 1972, I made the decision to come to the University of Victoria to finish my university degree. I was working in Nanaimo at the time, teaching swimming and lifeguarding at the Nanaimo public pool. On one of my rare weekends off, I came to Victoria looking for a place to live, so I went to the University housing office and received a list of people who had rooms to rent. On that list were Pat and Phil Williamson, who had a small room to rent in their basement. Their name just seemed to jump out at me. When I finally got to their house I saw Phil - the tallest man I'd ever seen - working on the side of their house. When I inquired about the room, in the usual Phil way he said: "Go, ask my wife." When I knocked, the door opened and there was Pat speaking on a telephone with a twelve-foot cord, holding Benjamin, who was then three months old, while she herself was drinking a cup of coffee. She invited me into their house. My life has never been the same since. In August of 1974, I moved into their little room in the basement and stayed for four years. I needed a family and they had their prayer answered for someone to fill their room.

Memorial Stone 3: Part of my rental arrangement was to have my meals provided. Pat and Phil talked to me at mealtimes about the love of Christ. Not only did they give thanks for their food, but they regularly talked about the Lord and what he was doing in their lives. I was rough, hard and my language was awful. Pat had decided that if I didn't change she was going to ask me to leave ... then the Lord intervened.

The Church of God in Victoria was having a series of prophecy meetings with Jack Ferguson, Reg. Darke, and Bob Armstrong. It was being held in a hall not far from the pool. Pat suggested that I come to a meeting. I walked into the hall with wet hair, dressed in sweatpants and sweatshirt only to see women in hats, all dressed up and men in suits and ties. As the meeting went on, Mr Ferguson came to Rev.14:19-20, *the angel swung his sickle to the earth, and gathered the clusters from the vine of the earth, and threw them into the great winepress of the wrath of God. And the winepress was trodden outside the city, and blood came up from the winepress, up to the horse's bridle, for a distance of 200 miles.*

I was terrified. I felt at that very moment Armageddon was going to happen. As I was preparing to leave the hall, Mr Ferguson cornered me and asked me if I knew the Lord as my Saviour. I said, "No," ducked under his arm, jumped on my bike, and rode home - fast!

When I got home, I went right to my room and I stayed there. For the entire night I paced my room. I couldn't rest. At 6 am, I knelt beside my bed and said, "God, if you are real, I need to know it." His audible reply was: "I have been waiting, now is the day of salvation." At that moment, it was as if the weight of sin - and all the desperation in my life - lifted from my shoulders. In the morning when I went up for breakfast, Pat knew immediately that I'd had an encounter with the Lord. She said she now knew what the face of Moses must have been like when he came down from the mountain! The most telling difference, however, was the change in the words that came from my mouth. I certainly knew that a real transaction had taken place.

In the summer of 1974 I went, for the first time, to Britain. There, I met Jack Ferguson and we had a long conversation, during which I learned that Jack had also been spoken to audibly by the Lord. On his way to Canada that year, he had prayed fervently while flying that there might be a soul saved. During the meeting, just as I walked in, he told me the Lord said to him: "There's your soul, don't let her get away." Jack told me that he'd never cornered anyone before or since, but that he knew this was his opportunity. I will be forever grateful for the Lord bringing these people into my life to lead me to the Lord. The unique thing to me was that once I started reading the Scriptures there was never a doubt as to where I would worship. I saw the hedged garden, and God's house within, and I knew that was for me. In January of 1975 I was added to the Church of God in Victoria.

NT: It's surely unusual how personal guidance was obtained in these instances. We understand that teaching which is for all of us to obey is contained solely in God's Word carefully understood in its context. Did you have one more memorial stone for us, Sue?

Memorial Stone 4: When I was 31 years old I met a young man with whom I wanted to have a relationship. I prayed desperately to the Lord over a number of months, but seemed to get no answers. As Jeff and I continued to write, e-mail and meet, we were at a place where we would have to decide whether to take our relationship to the next level. He was everything I wanted in a man: kind, gentle, strong, dependable, someone with whom I could have children. As I continued to pray to God, I felt no nearer to an answer. I pleaded with God to let me know what I should do. I could not imagine my life without children, a husband, a home and all the things that little girls dream of. After three months of trying to decide what I should do, the Lord gave me a verse: *For your husband is your Maker, whose name is the Lord of hosts.* [2] He gave me this five different times through different people or readings. Jeff and I chatted over the period of a week, and I finally had the courage to tell him that I thought our relationship wasn't going to go further. Although disappointed, he understood. I cried for days. So I have been called to singleness. Do I like it? Most of the time, I do.

NT: *Thanks for sharing your story with us. It's a good thing to give thanks to the Lord for his wonderful interventions in our lives, as the psalmist did. The recollection of what God has done in our lives, strengthens our trust in Him for whatever lies ahead.*

References: (1) Josh.4:7 (2) Isa.54:5

Bible quotations from NASB

MISSION: CAMP WORK (RICHARD HUTCHINSON)

This summer marked my 25th year of being at camps in Northern Ireland and when I packed up this year after our Mixed Week, adding it all up I had completed my 50th camp. Should the Lord spare me, I hope to add a good many more to that total - though I doubt I'll reach my century - but this article is not a raising of one's bat toward the pavilion; it is a reflection on what camp work is all about and why it is such a valuable avenue of our outreach activities in Churches of God.

A little history first, for which I'm indebted to J.J. Park's account of *The Churches of God: Their Origin and Development in the 20th Century*. It was Dr. Charles Luxmoore who ran our first camps from his own home in Halifax back in 1907 and 1908. Dr. Luxmoore's desire was for young people from different churches of God to study the Word together 'so that they would appreciate the value of fellowship and friendship in the things of God'. Since those early years there have been camps in the UK every year except when the Second World War interrupted things in 1940-41. After the war-time hiatus, UK camps started up in earnest again, with girls included for the first time and, from 1946 onwards, UK camps were held in several districts rather than as one national affair. The late '40s also saw camps beginning in Canada, America and Australia.

So, from then until now, camp-work has grown into one of the cornerstones of our outreach work, and it is a thrilling and rewarding work to be involved in. The original intention of Dr. Luxmoore is still at the heart of why we are running camps for young disciples today, and of course, there is a strong Gospel mission at the heart of our work with younger boys and girls. For those who are involved with the young people of camps, and for those who support with prayer and their finances, camp is a precious work, more than worthy of the demands it lays upon us.

What is it that makes camp work so special? I think a large part of it is that camp presents a unique opportunity for us to build stronger relationships with the children we work with. Instead of seeing them for an hour or so once a week, at camp we spend every waking moment of a full week with them. You get to know the boys and girls as individuals. You build bridges with them and hopefully build trust, so that they begin to see you as someone genuinely interested in them and their welfare. When camp is over, those 'one hour, once a week' youth club sessions have value added by time invested with the children in camps.

Time at camp is time away from distractions and, in many cases, distressing situations. Some of the children have home lives we can scarcely imagine, and very worldly environments. Simply removing them from that milieu has a big impact in itself- I've often seen youngsters who cause real problems at youth club seem much more agreeable after a day or two at camp, which shows just how important background influences can be. The camp environment is a unique opportunity to present a sustained programme of the Gospel, where the seed can be sown and then nurtured. It's not a quick 10-minute message and then off home until next week - it's hearing the Word of God a couple of times a day, singing songs about Jesus, giving thanks before every meal for Jesus, holding conversations with workers about Jesus. The campers can ask questions and get answers, and there is time for them to think over the things they learn.

Over the years, the Holy Spirit has worked consistently, wonderfully and mightily in the hearts of young boys and girls through camp work, and the full reaping of that harvest we'll not truly know until we see faces we never thought to see in 'the glory' - in the age to come. We have seen a renewed focus in the last 15-20 years on camps run for young Christians, which was Dr. Luxmoore's original intention. I'm certainly thankful that we began a Mixed Week here in Northern Ireland just as I turned 15 years of age. I benefited a great deal from both the times of study (which to me were a new experience at that time) and ministry. Where else might I have had the opportunity to spend that amount of time, at that age, engaged in getting to grips with God's Word?

I also formed many friendships with other young people from across the UK and further afield. The value of close friends who share your enthusiasm for the Lord's service has been proved to me countless times, and camp has furnished me with many who have encouraged and sustained me over the years. It is a very special thing to me to now be running camps and seeing young people form those same bonds of friendship; I can chart their spiritual development from year to year as they respond to the discussion groups and ministry sessions. 1 look at these young Christians and pray that I am looking at the future of the Fellowship of Churches of God and I count it a privilege to encourage their growth, even as I am encouraged by them growing.

Dr. Luxmoore would, I'm sure, be delighted to see exactly that end result he hoped for in 1907 now being borne out of camps all over the world in the Churches of God today. May God continue to glorify Himself in the salvation of young souls and the adding of young disciples to churches of God.

WOMEN PREACHERS? (BRIAN JOHNSTON)

The Bible states[1] that women are not permitted to speak when the church gathers together as a church. It is not given to women to lead the church in any audible, authoritative way. This agrees with what we find in 1 Tim.2:11 -12 - a *woman must quietly receive instruction ...I do not allow a woman to teach.* Yet, quite evidently, many believers throughout the denominations today consider this not to be the case. Let's examine some reasons why some have come to this conclusion:

Claim 1: "This text (1 Cor.14:34-35) is not authentic." However, the text appears in all known manuscripts. It would be irresponsible to try to minimize the force of these verses by doubting that they are original when no manuscript that has come down to us supports the case for their omission.

Claim 2: "The text is not as clear-cut as it appears to be." There have been attempts to play down the force of the statement, even though *they are not allowed to speak takes* the form of an absolute rule. Some, while agreeing that 1 Cor.14:34-35 is both authentic and absolute in character, limit its application to the evaluation of prophecies only. They do this by seeing this as part of a continuing instruction from the preceding verses. Paul's point here, they tell us, is that the women may not participate in the oral weighing up of such prophecies as he has been dealing with in the immediate context. But does it not seem inconsistent for those who claim that Paul permits women to audibly prophesy in a church gathering to also say that he forbids them the seemingly lesser task of weighing up the prophecies?

The clearer point is that these women were in learning mode,[2] and not undertaking any critical or editorial function with regard to freshly-delivered prophecies. For Paul is at pains to ensure that the restriction which he is making does not mean that the women cannot learn. This implies that it was a learning activity in which they were engaged, not the activity of publicly weighing up prophecies.

Paul's summing up actually begins at verse 26 when he proceeds to give practical guidelines for the ordering of both the gifts of tongues and prophesying when the early New Testament churches assembled together. Various in-church speaking roles are then listed in terms of exclusively masculine pronouns until Paul begins to address the womenfolk in verse 34, and then it is in order to explicitly confirm that they are indeed not permitted to speak.

Claim 3: But then, what of 1 Cor.11:5? In what sense is the woman there praying or prophesying? The only possible reconciliation with the praying and prophesying women of 11:5 is to understand these women as being part of the overall church company which was engaged in praying and prophesying, but which they specifically were not permitted to lead audibly.[3] After all, we today would not hesitate to similarly describe women present at the Breaking of the Bread as collectively worshipping (although silent), being equally part of the holy priesthood.

Claim 4: "This text only applies at that time to Corinth." This argues that the reasons behind Paul's demand for silence are local, probably cultural. The suggestion that some of these women were noisy (or uneducated) cannot be taken seriously, for we must surely ask why, in that case, does Paul ban **all** women from talking - and were there no noisy men? Since Paul's rule operates 'in all the churches' (vv.33b-34), it would be necessary to assume that all first-century Christian women were noisy which is obviously nonsensical.

Some think Paul was advocating a practice unique to Corinth, which means we can legitimately ignore it. Nothing could be further from the truth, Corinth was being asked to come into line with what all the other New Testament churches were already doing. *Has [the word of God] come to you only?*[4] Paul asks if they are not troubled by the fact that all the other churches have put the same instruction into a quite different ecclesiastical practice.

A further argument against this being a statement that speaks to that local culture only is the observation that they are not allowed to speak *as the law says*. By this, Paul is probably referring to the creation order in Gen.2:20b-24, for it is to there that Paul explicitly turns on two other occasions when he discusses female roles in a way which agrees with what we find here.[5] The verse in Genesis does not mention silence, but it does indicate that man was made first and woman was made for man, and a pattern has been laid down regarding the roles which the two play.

Bible quotations from NASB

References: (1) 1 Cor.14:34 (2) 1 Cor.14:35 (3) It is a fact that the Spirit gave prophecy to women to speak, even publicly (Acts 21:9; Lk.2:36-38), but not when the church was called together. The 1 Cor.14 portion which begins at v.26 gives an in-church context that is emphasized for sisters in v.33-35. (4) 1 Cor.14:36b (5) 1 Cor.11:8-9; 1 Tim.2:13

CONFLICT AT CORINTH: (1) CULTURAL TENSION (MARTIN JONES)

If you ever got the idea that the early churches of God ran like clockwork then you would be absolutely right. Unlike quartz timepieces, they needed a lot of maintenance and attention, were prone to coming to a complete halt and were even at risk of total breakdown! There's no better case study of it than the Church of God in Corinth, especially as it shows that the apostle Paul wasn't shock-proof either.

First century Corinth was a ready-made seedbed for church conflict. It was even the scene of a mythical territorial dispute between Poseidon, the god of the sea, and Helios, the god of the sun, which was resolved by allocating half of Corinth to one and half to the other.

Over the course of this year, with the aim of learning lessons for today, we're going to look at four types of conflict that this Church faced, either internally or from the outside:

- Cultural - existing and changing norms.
- Social - divisions in the church, social/economic inequalities and leadership battles.
- Moral - the gulf between Corinth's sexual standards and those of God.
- Pastoral - discipline, distrust and defensiveness.

Cultural conflict was exacerbated by Corinth being both very cosmopolitan and, in relative terms, very modern. Julius Caesar had only re-formed Corinth as a Roman colony less than a century before the Church was planted and it was populated mainly by indigenous Greeks, 'invading' Romans and Jews (like Priscilla and Aquila) fleeing from persecution at home. Each brought their own religions, languages, traditions and very different ways of thinking to the melting pot. An analysis of the membership of the Corinthian church reflects this diversity. Of the seventeen saints we know of, eight, like Gaius, have Latin names, Apollos and Crispus were Jews, while Stephanas and his family were Greek. It's not hard to imagine that this would have contributed to conflict at times.

Corinth was a major urban centre on the trade route in Greece and was known for being much more liberal culturally than the old-fashioned villages around it. It had also a reputation for being very expensive - the poet Horace (famous for the phrase *'carpe diem'*) said that 'not everyone is able to go to Corinth'. Space was at a premium, with density estimated to be on a par with today's shanty towns in Rio or Delhi - most people lived quite literally on top of each other in apartments above shops. Gaius must have been a wealthy man indeed to own a home large enough for the entire church to meet in.

Religion was definitely a huge cultural issue. It was common in worshipping certain Greek gods to invite friends to eat some of the meat sacrificed to the idol at a banquet, often in the god's temple (think of it as a first century business lunch). This situation was reflected in 1 Cor.8:10. Although the saints now knew that idol worship was strictly prohibited, there was a temptation to continue a basic part of the social life that they had enjoyed pre-conversion. Some had no problem with it but others certainly did. Paul had to advise very carefully on how best to deal with these sensitivities.

And, though we might be shocked to think of a saint being drunk when attending the Lord's Supper (see 1 Cor.11:21), this wasn't unusual. Drunkenness was sometimes considered a part of a religious rite, especially in the worship of Dionysus, the discoverer of wine. But this was in direct conflict with their new way of life and it had to be dispensed with, as Paul made clear. Each age and society has its distinct culture to be grappled with and if we're not conscious of a personal struggle then alarm bells should be ringing. Our response to it should be fashioned by the unchanging Word of God and not the other way around. Even so, what response is appropriate may not always be immediately apparent and so lengthy and prayerful consideration and taking advice from experienced brothers and sisters is always a good approach.

There are at least three courses of action available to us:

- Abandon - some cultural baggage may be best left abandoned entirely to better embrace the new culture of Christ or simply to avoid the risk of seriously stumbling a fellow Christian.
- Accept - it would be premature to conclude that everything in the world is automatically bad for us. God has provided many things for us to enjoy and to rule out harmless activities could hamper our testimony.
- Adapt - some culture can be adapted or harnessed to make it palatable and it can, with some finesse, even be turned into a witness opportunity.

Source references:

Dr. Bruce W. Winter, After Paul Left Corinth - The Influence of Secular Ethics and Social Change; Wayne A. Meeks, The First Urban Christians - The Social World of the Apostle Paul; Prof. Abraham Malherbe, Social Aspects of Early Christianity

CONFLICT AT CORINTH: (2) SOCIAL TENSIONS (ALEX REID)

Corinth was an important centre of trade and commerce in New Testament times and we find the social divisions that we would expect; from the day labourer to the wealthy business person; from those high on the social status ladder to the very lowest. Perhaps this is reflected in Paul's description of the Corinthian church: *For consider your calling, brethren, that there were not many wise according to the flesh, ... not many noble.* [1] In saying *not many,* the apostle did not say 'not any', for it is evident in reading Corinthians that there were some people of substance within the church. Another social division that existed in Corinth was that between slave and free,[2] such were the normal social divisions of those days. But there existed in the church at Corinth divisions that were unexpected in a community based on mutual love and respect. These were party factions, lawsuits among saints and a flaunting of wealth by some.

Party factions within the church were caused by allegiance to one prominent person over another: *... there are quarrels among you. Now I mean this, that each one of you is saying, "I am of Paul, " and "I of Apollos, " and "I of Cephas, " and "I of Christ".*[3] Such entrenched positions were little better than the partisan politics of the secular world: *... are you not walking like mere men?*[4] In accusing them of acting like 'mere men', Paul may have been comparing their behaviour to that of the disciples of the sophist teachers of the time. These professional teachers, debaters and public speakers sought to gather groups of followers, and their secular disciples were often openly competitive.[5]

It is hard to imagine one brother in the Lord taking another to court, but this was happening in Corinth.[6] It was common then for disputes among elite members of Corinthian society to spill over into the civil courts, and some among the Corinthian saints may have been following this cultural practice of settling their differences.[7] Whatever the reason. Paul's condemnation of this practice is scathing: *I say this to your shame. Is it so that there is not among you one wise man who will be able to decide between his brethren, but brother goes to law with brother, and that before unbelievers?*[8]

There were serious problems at the gatherings of the church, particularly in connection with the Breaking of Bread, or Lord's Supper. Some were making this gathering an occasion for excess and indulging themselves in food and drink.[9] The effect of this excess was the severe embarrassment of the saints who had little or nothing: *Or do you despise the church of God and shame those who have nothing? What shall I say to you? Shall I praise you? In this I will not praise you.*[10]

Having noted some of the conflicts at Corinth, we need to ask what the root cause was. The apostle identifies a major cause as arrogance: *Now some have become arrogant ... and I shall find out, not the words of those who are arrogant but their power.*[11] Arrogance breeds boasting and feelings of superiority: *For who regards you as superior? What do you have that you did not receive? And if you did receive it, why do you boast as if you had not received it?*[12]

What did these feelings of arrogance and superiority spring from? Corinth was a highly gifted church.[13] Their over-emphasis on spiritual gifts and knowledge, to the exclusion of more important things was their undoing: *Knowledge makes arrogant, but love edifies.*[14] It was to this gifted, but dysfunctional, church that the great apostle wrote that wonderful passage about love: *Love is patient, love is kind and is not jealous; love does not brag and is not arrogant, does not act unbecomingly;*

it does not seek its own, is not provoked, does not take into account a wrong suffered ...[15] Surely here was the answer to the problems at Corinth, and to many of the problems in Christian communities today; spiritual knowledge and gifts, decoupled from love, takes us in a wholly undesirable direction.

References: (1) 1 Cor.1:26 (2) 1 Cor.7:22 (3) 1 Cor.1:11-12 (4) 1 Cor.3:3-4 (5) Bruce W. Winter, After Paul left Corinth: The Influence of Secular Ethics and Social Change, Eerdmans Publishing Co. 2001, p.31-43 (6) 1 Cor.6:7-8 (7) Bruce W. Winter, After Paul left Corinth p.58-75 (8) 1 Cor.6:5-6 (9) 1 Cor.11:20-22 (10) 1 Cor.11:22 (11) 1 Cor.4:18-19 (12) 1 Cor.4:7 (13) 1 Cor.1:5-7 (14) 1 Cor.8:1 (15) 1 Cor.13:4-5

Bible quotes from NASB

CONFLICT AT CORINTH: (3) MORAL ISSUES (GEOFF HYDON)

Growing up in the Midlands of the UK (in the 1950s) it was not uncommon to hear from one's parents: "They may do that there anywhere else, but you'll not do that there here!" What was reportedly permitted in a friend's house did not make the same behaviour acceptable at home. You can almost hear this sentiment from Paul's lips as he guided the young church of God in Corinth. What might be accepted in their culture was nevertheless very inappropriate for them now as God's church.

As a major port, the population of Corinth would include many immigrants, business people and travellers, away from home and family influence. It had previously in its history become a place notorious for its lax morals, and 'corinthianize' had become a term referring to sexual impurity. To see how challenging the cultural setting was in Corinth, first read Paul's letter to the Romans. Remember, he wrote it from Corinth.[1] Surely things that were so upsetting to Paul in the Roman colony of Corinth would underlie some of his comments to saints in Rome itself. So read Romans again (especially the first few chapters), remember how history repeats itself, reflect on Paul's surroundings in Corinth. Then think of your own cities and towns today.

Today, the culture around us may reflect popular assumptions that: marriage should *follow* sexual experimentation;[2] monogamy is unnecessary;[3] divorce is inevitable;[4] same-sex unions are acceptable choices;[5] drinking for fun (or use of hallucinogenic drugs in minor amounts) is normal;[6] abortion and euthanasia are just personal choices;[7] in the 'me' generation self-interest trumps altruism;[8] petty theft is inconsequential;[9] cheating on taxes or other similar lies is OK;[10] gambling is a positive contributor to society.[11] To the sanctified mind most of these fall under Paul's statement, that such things should *not even be named among you.*[12] But you and I are pressured every day by a surrounding culture like Corinth's that argues such things are really acceptable, and even wise. Check the footnotes to find the Spirit's counter instruction through Paul.

A convenient medium to express the local culture in Corinth was what we might term graffiti. Slogans of competing philosophers were written boldly in public places for all to see. They were like the 'tweets' used today to spread personal views. Similarly we can see the use of popular philosophy in the slogans the Corinthians used: 'Everything is permissible';[13] 'Foods for the stomach and the stomach for foods',[14] which in their cultural setting were sayings employed to justify satisfying their sexual and physical appetites. Such things typified the feasts arranged by Roman citizens, and it seems some thought this 'freedom' extended to excusing misbehaviour in the church.[15] Similar warped logic led some to focus on a so-called 'spirituality' that allowed them to ignore sinful use of their bodies, thinking their souls would be unaffected![16] Paul evidently had an uphill battle to correct errors spawned by the encroaching culture. Does it sound familiar?

Paul's Spirit-led instruction to Corinthian saints was to show them a much higher and contrasting standard.[17] He used popular quotes himself to reinforce practical warnings.[18] He refuted earthly wisdom expressed by philosophers and contrasted it with the wisdom of God.[19] God's wisdom is expressed in sacrificial and selfless giving. Therefore, any thought that all things were permissible must be strongly qualified.[20] Actions must be God-glorifying,[21] and focused on what is helpful to others not just gratifying to oneself, even if that requires strict self-control.[22] The ultimate response to their self-serving arguments was to consider the reality of bodily resurrection, and the far-reaching consequences of that unavoidable fact for all people.[23] Is it therefore surprising that in today's debates about Christianity and its true values, it is the essential belief in the resurrection that drives hearers to draw definite conclusions, just as it did for Greeks centuries ago in Corinth, and Athens too?[24]

References: (1) Rom.16:23; 1 Cor.1:14 (2) 1 Cor.6:13-20; 1 Cor.10:8 (3) 1 Cor.7:2 (4) 1 Cor.7:10 (5) 1 Cor.6:9 (6) 1 Cor.5:11; 2 Cor.7:1 and see 1 Thess.5:8 (7) 1 Cor.6:19 and see Ps.139:13-16 regarding the sanctity of the human body (8) 1 Cor.10:24,33 & 1 Cor.8:13 (9) 1 Cor.6:10 (10) 1 Cor.5:8; 1 Cor.13:6 and see 2 Tim.3:13 (11) 1 Cor.5:11; 1 Cor.6:10 gambling often reflects covetousness (12) Eph.5:3 (13) 1 Cor.6:12; 1 Cor.10:23 Gk: Πάντα ἔξεστιν 'All things are lawful' (NKJV) (14) 1 Cor.6:13 (15) 1 Cor.11:20-22; 2 Cor.12:21 (16) 1 Cor.3:1; 1 Cor.6:13-15; 1 Cor.14:37 (17) 2 Cor.6:14-7:1 (18) 1 Cor.15:32,33 (19) 1 Cor.1:20-31 (20) 1 Cor.6:12 (21) 1 Cor.10:31 (22) 1 Cor.10:23-24 & 1 Cor.9:27 (23) 1 Cor.15:32-34; 50-58 (24) Acts 17:31-32

CONFLICT AT CORINTH: (4) PASTORAL CONFLICT (LEONARD ROSS)

'Pastoral conflict' - two words which do not sit comfortably together, especially in the context of a church of God. Those in the Church of God in Corinth are described as being *sanctified in Christ Jesus and called ... saints.* [1] By God's grace they were enriched in knowledge, had the ability to communicate well, and were not lacking in gift; they eagerly anticipated the coming of the Lord; terms which should be descriptive of every church of God, then and now. What a pleasure it should be to 'pastor' such a group of disciples!

Sadly, the reality was that the spiritual standing of the Corinthian church was not reflected in its daily life. Whilst Paul was with them,[2] they were comparatively safe, and might have been better able to resist returning to their former way of life, but now in his absence it seems the 'flesh' was asserting itself once more. News from Chloe's household of divisions, quarrelling,[3] gross and unchecked sinful practice, brings great distress to Paul who, with Apollos, was a spiritual father to them, and who had, with godly jealousy, presented the church to Christ as a *pure virgin.* His fear was that the minds of these his spiritual children were being *led astray from a sincere and pure devotion to Christ.* [4] Though they might have ten thousand tutors in Christ, all the instruction in the world without the caring affection of spiritual fathers to help apply it, would be unproductive in this young and immature church. Where were their elders and shepherds?

'Pastoring' from a distance will never be easy or effective, especially if the flock has little confidence in its shepherd, and this sadly was something which greatly disturbed Paul. It seems that, to some, he was just not acceptable, and they questioned his apostleship and sought to undermine his God-given authority. In his second epistle to Corinth he is compelled to defend this and indulge in boasting to vindicate his character and ministry. His reluctance at doing this surely displays a humility befitting such a great pastor amongst the people of God of that day. In the meantime, however, he sees the need of the personal touch, and so he tells them he is sending Timothy to remind them of his *ways in Christ, as I teach them .. in every church.* [5]

The choice would be theirs - would he come to them with a rod. or in that spirit of love and gentleness which pleads with them.[6] To the man who daily felt such deep concern for all the churches, would Corinth become an even greater burden?[7] The communication from Chloe along, possibly, with verbal reports from Stephanas, Fortunatus and Achaicus[8] seeks advice on a number of practical difficulties, and in this first epistle Paul deals with these. Of major concern, of course, are the divisions within the church, for a house divided against itself cannot stand.[9] It seems unlikely that Apollos or Peter would have welcomed such followings and Paul certainly did not; he tells them in effect to 'grow up' and not behave like immature and worldly children - they are 'God's temple' in whom the Spirit of God dwells.[10] They should remember their calling[11] and *let no one boast in men. For all things are yours, whether Paul or Apollos or Cephas ... you are Christ's...*[12] The leaders were simply *servants of Christ and stewards of the mysteries of God,*[13] *God's fellow workers*[14] answerable to the one whom Peter would one day describe as the Chief Shepherd.[15]

Whilst we may deprecate the problems in Corinth, without them we would not have these two great epistles. How much poorer we all would be without the gem of 1 Cor.13! But those who today have pastoral responsibility as elders in the churches of God, will one day be called to 'give account', as also will Paul. What will he say about Corinth? And what will those who watch out for our souls say? May we allow them to do this with joy and not with grief, for that would be unprofitable for us.[16]

Bible quotations from the ESV

References: (1) 1 Cor.1:2 (2) Acts 18 (3) 1 Cor.1:11 (4) 2 Cor.11:2-3 (5)1 Cor.4:17 (6) 1 Cor.4:21; 2 Cor.10:1 (7) 2 Cor.11:28 (8) 1 Cor.16:17 (9) Mk.3:25 (10) 1 Cor.3:16 (11) 1 Cor.1:26 (12) 1 Cor.3: 21-23 (13) 1 Cor.4:1 (14) 1 Cor.3:9 (15) 1 Pet.5:4 (16) Heb.13:17

GOSSIP (EDWIN NEELY)

The Old English word was *godsibb,* a friendly term describing relatives and close friends, and eventually describing the chatter of women gathered to assist in childbirth. The word was first used as a verb by Shakespeare, but its present meaning is quite different, involving the idle and often meaningfully hurtful slanted anecdote that flies on wings of quicksilver and leaves destruction in its path. Solomon described the action as *going down into the inmost body.* [1] and he didn't mean with any good results. Paul condemns the actions of such as engage in this hurtful practice: *... idle ... gossips and busybodies, saying things which they ought not.* [2] A few in his day were guilty of it; I wonder what he would say if he lived in our time!

Marshall McLuhan described modern gadgets as having become extensions of the human body - the typewriter of the fingers, the bicycle of the legs, the telephone of the ears, and so on. Were he alive today he might expand that thought exponentially. Today, modern gadgetry means we don't even have to wander about from house to house spreading rumours; we can accelerate the practice with the extension of thumb action. We are accountable for the words of our mouths; [3] we are no less accountable for the action of our thumbs and fingers! James warns us well: *If anyone does not stumble in word, he is a perfect man, able also to bridle the whole body ... And the tongue is afire, a world of iniquity ... it defiles ...* [4] Of course the tongue defiles in many ways, but we need remember that one of them is gossip, whether oral or electronically transmitted!

Among dedicated believers gossip at times disguises itself in the camouflage of "matters for prayer", human interest for supposedly good intent, but nonetheless hurtful in its broadcast. It begins with statements like, "I'm very concerned about ... (you fill in the name)." There are times to speak, but there are times when we need to learn to be silent. One wise man taught his son, "Never overlook the opportunity to keep your mouth shut!" Even prayer meetings should not be used as platforms for gossip. Some things need be prayed about, certainly, but on one's knees, alone with the One who knows all things already.[5]

God's law through Moses to Israel was: *"You shall not go about as a talebearer among your people ... I am the LORD. "*[6] To this Solomon adds. *A talebearer reveals secrets, but he who is of a faithful spirit conceals a matter.* [7] and adds in Prov.26 that though a talebearer's words are like tasty trifles they cause strife. To the Thessalonian saints Paul exhorts that those who walk in a disorderly manner as busybodies should learn to work in quietness.[8] As well as spreading gossip there is the possibility of feeding on it. Modern media have made celebrity gossip popular and acceptable in our society. No matter what dirt is cast up in the lives of sports stars, celebrities or politicians it becomes a delightful titbit for public consumption on a world-wide scale. Nothing seems taboo; all is open and laid bare - and it defiles!

The Christian believer needs no part of it. Gossip is social sewage; it rots the spirit! The Holy Spirit advises us rather to think on things which are true, noble, just. pure, lovely, of good report, things of virtue and praiseworthy.[9] The Lord Jesus knew all things, He knew what was in man, but He didn't talk about it, nor did He advise the spread of that kind of news. He should be our example in word as well as action. He did not gossip; can we who are His afford or even want to do so?

Bible quotations from NKJV

References: (1) Prov.18:8; 26:22 (2) 1 Tim.5:13 (3) Matt.12:36 (4) Jas.3:2,6 (5) Matt.6:6 (6) Lev.19:16 (7) Prov.11:13 (8) 2 Thess.3:11-12 (9) Phil.4:8

Also by Hayes Press

Bible Studies
Bible Studies 1990 - First Samuel
Bible Studies 1991 - The First Letter of Paul to the Corinthians
Bible Studies 1993 - Second Samuel
Bible Studies 1994 - The Establishment and Development of Churches of God
Bible Studies 1995 - The Kings of Judah and Israel from Solomon to Asa
Bible Studies 1992 - The Second Letter of Paul to the Corinthians

Needed Truth
Needed Truth 1888
Needed Truth 2001
Needed Truth 2002
Needed Truth 2003
Needed Truth 2004
Needed Truth 2005
Needed Truth 2006
Needed Truth 2007
Needed Truth 2008
Needed Truth 2009
Needed Truth 2010

Needed Truth 2011
Needed Truth 2012
Needed Truth 2015
Needed Truth 1888-1988: A Centenary Review of Major Themes

Standalone
The Road Through Calvary: 40 Devotional Readings
Lovers of God's House
Different Discipleship: Jesus' Sermon on the Mount
The House of God: Past, Present and Future
The Kingdom of God
Knowing God: His Names and Nature
Churches of God: Their Biblical Constitution and Functions
Four Books About Jesus
Collected Writings On ... Exploring Biblical Fellowship
Collected Writings On ... Exploring Biblical Hope
Collected Writings On ... The Cross of Christ
Builders for God
Collected Writings On ... Exploring Biblical Faithfulness
Collected Writings On ... Exploring Biblical Joy
Possessing the Land: Spiritual Lessons from Joshua
Collected Writings On ... Exploring Biblical Holiness
Collected Writings On ... Exploring Biblical Faith
Collected Writings On ... Exploring Biblical Love
These Three Remain...Exploring Biblical Faith, Hope and Love
The Teaching and Testimony of the Apostles
Pressure Points - Biblical Advice for 20 of Life's Biggest Challenges
More Than a Saviour: Exploring the Person and Work of Jesus
The Psalms: Volumes 1-4 Boxset
The Faith: Outlines of Scripture Doctrine
Key Doctrines of the Christian Gospel

Is There a Purpose to Life?
An Introduction to Bible Covenants
The Hidden Christ - Volume 2: Types and Shadows in Offerings and Sacrifices
The Hidden Christ Volume 1: Types and Shadows in the Old Testament
The Hidden Christ - Volume 3: Types and Shadows in Genesis
Heavenly Meanings - The Parables of Jesus
Fisherman to Follower: The Life and Teaching of Simon Peter
Called to Serve: Lessons from the Levites
Needed Truth 2017 Issue 1
The Breaking of the Bread: Its History, Its Observance, Its Meaning
Great Spiritual Revivals
An Introduction to the Book of Hebrews
The Holy Spirit and the Believer
Exploring The Psalms: Volume 1 - Thoughts on Key Themes
Exploring The Psalms: Volume 2 - Exploring Key Elements
Exploring the Psalms: Volume 3 - Surveying Key Sections
The Psalms: Volume 4 - Savouring Choice Selections
Profiles of the Prophets
The Hidden Christ - Volumes 1-4 Box Set
The Hidden Christ - Volume 4: Types and Shadows in Israel's Tabernacle
Baptism - Its Meaning and Teaching
Conflict and Controversy in the Church of God in Corinth
In the Shadow of Calvary: A Bible Study of John 12-17
Moses: God's Deliverer
Sparkling Facets: Bible Names and Titles of Jesus
A Little Book About Being Christlike
Keys to Church Growth
From Shepherd Boy to Sovereign: The Life of David
Back to Basics: A Study of Core Bible Teaching and Practice
An Introduction to the Holy Spirit

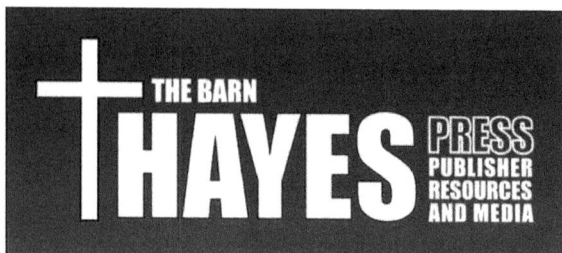

About the Publisher

Hayes Press (www.hayespress.org) is a registered charity in the United Kingdom, whose primary mission is to disseminate the Word of God, mainly through literature. It is one of the largest distributors of gospel tracts and leaflets in the United Kingdom, with over 100 titles and hundreds of thousands despatched annually. In addition to paperbacks and eBooks, Hayes Press also publishes Plus Eagles Wings, a fun and educational Bible magazine for children, and Golden Bells, a popular daily Bible reading calendar in wall or desk formats. Also available are over 100 Bibles in many different versions, shapes and sizes, Bible text posters and much more!

www.ingramcontent.com/pod-product-compliance
Lightning Source LLC
Chambersburg PA
CBHW071534040426
42452CB00008B/1013